Mark Seaman was educated at Dulwich College and University of Liverpool, and is a historian on the staff of the Imperial War Museum. He has made a speciality of Intelligence and Special Operations during the Second World War. In 1984 he organized the exhibition *European Resistance to Nazi Germany*, and in 1995 completed work on the museum's major permanent gallery, *Secret War*. He has written extensively on the subject, including in *The Times* and the *Independent*; has acted as adviser to film and television productions, and is the author of *Bravest of the Brave*, a biography of the Special Operations Executive agent Wing Commander F F E Yeo-Thomas GC.

Ian Kershaw was educated at St Bede's College, Manchester, University of Liverpool and Merton College, Oxford. He is Professor of Modern History at the University of Sheffield. His works on Nazi Germany have been translated into a number of languages. His biography of Hitler will be published in two volumes by Penguin, the first in September 1998, and will appear simultaneously in German translation.

*Ministry of Information cartoon of Hitler
by Richard Ziegler* (PRO INF 3/1298)

OPERATION FOXLEY

The British Plan to Kill Hitler

Introduction by Mark Seaman

with a Foreword by Ian Kershaw

PUBLIC RECORD OFFICE

PRO Publications
Kew
Richmond
Surrey TW9 4DU

Crown Copyright 1998

ISBN 1 873 162 72 3

A catalogue card for this book
is available from the British Library

Photographs from the Public Record Office,
and courtesy of the Imperial War Museum, London

Printed in Great Britain
by Multiplex Medway Ltd, Walderslade, Kent

Contents

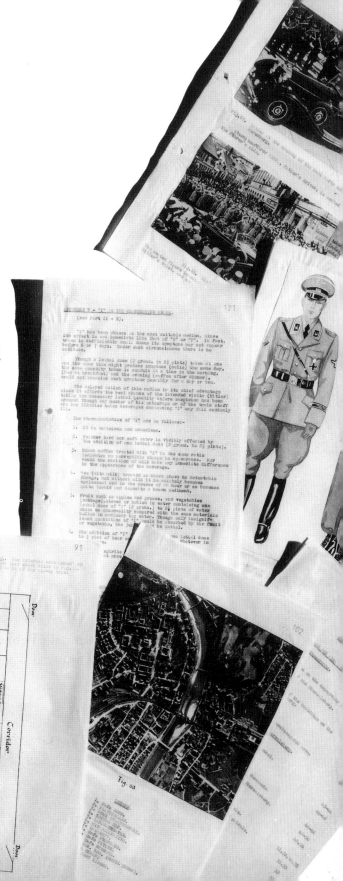

Foreword

It should probably have been no surprise that secret plans to assassinate Hitler (and a number of subordinate Nazi leaders) were mooted in Britain during the war. But it certainly *was* a surprise when the news of Operation FOXLEY broke. The sensation in the press showed how closely the secret had been guarded. There was surprise, too, at the extent and quality of SOE's intelligence on Hitler's surroundings and movements at his alpine retreat near Berchtesgaden, in southern Bavaria, and on his security arrangements. Some of this new information makes a notable addition to previous knowledge. The publication of the full dossier on FOXLEY is, therefore, greatly to be welcomed, above all for the intriguing insight it provides into thinking in top British intelligence circles during the last phase of the war and the possible methods of carrying out the assassination.

Among the most revealing papers in the files, in my view, are the conflicting assessments of the desirability of killing Hitler. SOE's senior staff officers were sharply divided in their views. The argument that killing Hitler would ensure his martyrdom in the eyes of the German population, and that his bungling war strategy (as SOE chiefs saw it) made him worth more alive than dead to the Allies, was countered by the view that the German war effort would collapse almost overnight if Hitler were eliminated. The varying responses of historians and other commentators to the papers on their release showed that widely differing interpretations still prevail more than half a century later.

How desirable it would have been to assassinate Hitler depends in some measure on the timing. According to one memorandum in the dossier, SOE had considered such a move in 1941, only – for reasons not disclosed – to discard the proposition. The killing of Hitler at that date

– though it is, in fact, doubtful in the extreme that it could have been accomplished – would have had seismic consequences for the course of the war. By late June 1944, when FOXLEY was seriously discussed for the first time, that was less clear. The Allied landing in Normandy had by then been successfully consolidated, though the advance was still slow and German resistance tenacious. In the East, the Red Army was making notable advances, even if a mighty struggle, ending in the streets of Berlin, still lay ahead. The war was far from over. But the days of the Hitler regime were plainly numbered. Allied strategy had long been targeted at the *total* defeat of Germany, embodied in the policy of 'unconditional surrender' proclaimed at the Casablanca Conference in January 1943. This aim was now in sight.

Of course, a successful assassination of Hitler *might* have helped realize that aim earlier than it was in fact attained, *might* have brought a more rapid end to the war. This would have spared much of the immense human misery and suffering which mounted drastically in the last months of the conflagration. The victims of the unbelievable inhumanity in the concentration camps would have been released from their torture much earlier. Many who succumbed in the last months would have lived. In Germany itself, the carnage in Dresden and other cities obliterated by Allied bombing in the final phase of the war would not have taken place. And the continuing enormous military losses on the Eastern and Western Fronts, including those resulting from the last great German offensive in the Ardennes, the 'Battle of the Bulge', initiated directly by Hitler, would have been avoided. The *potential* gains from an assassination of Hitler were, therefore, massive. Even without the advantage of hindsight into the magnitude of what might have been achieved, it is easy to see why some of the SOE chiefs were drawn to Operation FOXLEY.

But it is also possible that the killing of Hitler would not have accelerated the end of the war. Most probably, as other SOE strategists argued, a successful assassination by enemy forces (and, as was pointed out, this would inevitably have been recognized) would have brought an intense rallying round the cult of the 'martyred' Führer and a strengthening of the fanaticized minority of the population which remained, despite all setbacks, fervent and devoted believers in Hitler. Many of these had burnt their boats in the genocidal policies of the regime and would have been unlikely to throw away their arms unless some self-serving deal could have been struck with the Western Allies. Goering or, more probably, Himmler would most likely have taken over as the next leader. It is doubtful that power would have passed to the Wehrmacht. Most of the leading oppositional figures in the army had in any case been arrested, many of them killed, following the ill-fated Stauffenberg attempt on Hitler's life on 20 July 1944 (which had brought a big upsurge in support for the Führer). Many of the remaining generals were either Hitler-loyalists or politically supine. The most likely guess is that the war would have continued, at least for the time being, while the next leader tried to negotiate a peace separating the Western Allies from the Soviet Union – something the Nazi leadership had always strived for. If the Western Allies entertained such a separate peace – which would have been highly unlikely, and would have flown in the face of the 'unconditional surrender' policy with victory practically there for the taking – the breach with the Soviet Union would have come before it actually did; before, that is, a total defeat of Germany had been achieved. This would scarcely have altered the postwar balance of power in eastern Europe. But it might well have enhanced the prospect of more than just a 'Cold War' between East and West in the following years. Without such a separate peace, however, without, that is, negotiated terms leaving the Allies with less than the unconditional surrender they sought, it is not easy to see why the Germans, even without Hitler, would have seen an alternative to fighting on to the bitter end.

When that end inevitably did come, the task of rebuilding a democratic Germany would have been made immeasurably more difficult by a successful assassination of Hitler. As those SOE chiefs who opposed FOXLEY claimed, a new version of the stab-in-the-back legend that had poisoned politics in the Weimar Republic and shored up the myth that the German forces had not been militarily defeated would have persisted. As it was, according to public opinion surveys a quarter of those asked in West Germany in 1952 still thought well of Hitler, and a third opposed the attack on his life by the German Resistance in 1944. It takes little to imagine how easily, in the event of the SOE assassination plan proving successful, defeat could have been blamed within Germany on a cowardly assassination of the heroic Führer by enemy agents. Rebuilding Germany would have been all the harder with that allegation still lingering.

Actually, there was no question of a final decision having to be taken on whether to go ahead with FOXLEY. By the time the assassination plan had been fully devised, in spring 1945, the end of the war was imminent. FOXLEY, as SOE realized, had been overtaken by events. The point of any hazardous assassination attempt was by now even more dubious than it had been at the inception of the plan.

In fact, the timing and character of the feasibility studies of FOXLEY meant that the plan in any case never had a chance of being put into operation. All the designs for an assassination attempt were predicated on the attack taking place either at Hitler's residence at the Berghof – the huge complex surrounding his alpine residence on the Obersalzberg, above Berchtesgaden – or on his special train, while it was stationed in that area or travelling from that region. The meeting to instigate FOXLEY took place on 28 June. The plans were still under deliberation in early 1945. But Hitler left the Berghof on 14 July, never to return there. Scarcely two weeks existed, therefore, between the decision to put together a plan to kill Hitler and the last moment when that plan could have been executed. FOXLEY, it must be concluded, was defunct even before an operational plan could be put together.

Ian Kershaw
July 1998

Introduction

The threat of assassination was an everyday feature of Adolf Hitler's life from the beginning of his political career. In the years after the First World War, German politics bore an underlying current of violence and intimidation. Rival gangs not only battled in the streets but frequently carried out the assassination of their opponents, with the result that 376 political murders took place in Germany from 1919 to 1922. From his earliest days as leader of the Nazi Party, Hitler and his closest associates were aware of the need to insure his personal safety. There developed around him a complex and extensive bodyguard system which, by the time he became Chancellor in 1933, had become an

Hitler, closely followed by a cavalcade of bodyguards, makes a triumphal entry into Vienna, March 1938 (IWM MH 13129)

1

all but impenetrable cloak of protection. His security service was particularly effective at infiltrating opposition groups and nipping conspiracies in the bud. However, Hitler's regular public appearances made him a relatively easy target for potential assassins, and a leading authority (Hoffmann 1979) has estimated that more than thirty plots or actual attempts were made against Hitler's life by the outbreak of the war in September 1939.

Two of the assassination attempts that came closest to achieving success by penetrating Hitler's security involved a certain kind of individual: the loner. The first, Maurice Bavaud, was a Swiss theology student who in 1938 determined to assassinate Hitler. He made several preparatory trips to Germany, posing as an admirer of the Führer, but secretly investigating the best location at which to make his attempt. He visited Berlin and Hitler's retreat at Berchtesgaden in the Bavarian Alps, but found it impossible to keep track of his target's peripatetic schedule. Finally he decided to make his attempt in Munich during the annual ceremonies commemorating the abortive Nazi Putsch of 1923. Bavaud knew precisely where Hitler would be found and anticipated that the Nazi Old Guard's march through the streets would provide an ideal opportunity for the assassination. He managed to secure a ticket for one of the viewing stands on the route and, on 9 November 1938, armed with a pistol he had bought in Basle, was ready and waiting when Hitler and his entourage approached. But it transpired that the assassin's position near the procession did not allow him a clear shot because Hitler was obscured by attendants, SS and SA bodyguards. Undaunted, Bavaud continued to shadow Hitler, shuttling between Munich and Berchtesgaden but always finding that his quarry had eluded him. He was eventually obliged to give up the chase through lack of money and decided to return to his studies in France. But he was stopped and arrested while travelling without a ticket on a train bound for Augsburg. His pistol was discovered and, under interrogation by the Gestapo, he eventually confessed his plans. Bavaud was sentenced to death by the People's Court and beheaded in 1941.

A year later another even more dangerous assassin made an attempt on Hitler's life during the Munich ceremonies. Georg Elser, a cabinet maker with left-wing political beliefs, spent a year planning to plant a bomb in the Bürgerbräu Beer Hall where Hitler made an annual speech to Nazi Party veterans. Over an extended period of time Elser had stolen commercial explosives and, having moved to Munich, night after night excavated a secret niche in a stone pillar into which he put a sophisticated time bomb of his own design. On 8 November 1939 Hitler addressed his devoted followers in the Bürgerbräu. He started earlier than usual, made a briefer speech than in previous years, and left at 2107 hours. Therefore, when Elser's bomb detonated at 2120, killing eight people and wounding a further 60, Hitler was already on his way to the railway station. The failed assassin's luck was worse than that of his intended victim, and Elser was arrested that night while attempting to cross into Switzerland. He appears to have cooperated with his interrogators, and obligingly reconstructed his bomb as incontrovertible evidence of his guilt. Surprisingly, he was not tried and was only finally executed at Dachau

Hitler addressing his supporters at the Bürgerbräu beer hall shortly
before Georg Elser's bomb detonated, 8 November 1939
(IWM MH 13363)

concentration camp in April 1945. In consequence of Elser's bomb the Nazi security forces made a reassessment of Hitler's safety and in March 1940 new guidelines were laid down and procedures tightened.

Although the Gestapo were convinced that Elser had acted alone, there was much speculation in the German press that British Intelligence had been involved in the attempt. At the time of the Munich bomb, the Nazi Intelligence Service, the Sicherheitsdienst (SD), was running a sophisticated deception scheme in the Netherlands against representatives of the British Secret Intelligence Service (SIS). In a series of bogus negotiations, SD officers posed as members of a German Army opposition group seeking to overthrow Hitler. It is clear that the decision makers in London, in their innocence, were keen to develop these promising contacts, but the attempt on Hitler's life brought them to a violent conclusion. In large part to offset the evident failure of the

Ministry of Information cartoon
of Hitler by Richard Ziegler
(PRO INF 3/1296)

SS in maintaining Hitler's protection, Himmler ordered a riposte to the bombing. The day after the events in Munich, two SIS officers were lured to the Dutch–German border at Venlo where they were kidnapped by an SD snatch squad. Not only did the British agents' capture seriously damage SIS operations in western Europe, but the affair made Whitehall acutely suspicious of future overtures from Germans purporting to be opposed to Hitler.

There is no evidence to suggest that SIS was involved in any way with Elser's attempt on Hitler. In fact, evidence suggests that a conscious decision had been made to reject an earlier British assassination proposal. This scheme allegedly emanated in 1938 from Colonel F N Mason-MacFarlane, the British Military Attaché in Berlin. In a press interview in 1952, Mason-MacFarlane stated that he had been firmly convinced that Hitler's policies were drawing Europe into another war. He had therefore reported to London that, in the event of a failure to achieve a diplomatic solution to German aggrandisement, it would be possible to avert disaster by shooting the Nazi leader. He suggested that his Berlin residence offered an ideal vantage point for a clear sniper shot at Hitler while he stood on a reviewing stand during one of the numerous Berlin parades. The configuration of the apartment would allow the gunman to shoot from a position well away from the window and, especially if a silencer was used, the location from which the shot had been fired would be all but undetectible. If the suggestion ever achieved more than interested discussion and reached higher authority in Whitehall, the plan was turned down. (Mason-MacFarlane Papers, IWM MM 40)[1]

Thereafter, even after the outbreak of war in September 1939, the assassination of Hitler does not appear to have exercised the thoughts of the British military nor the government's secret agencies. However, in 1941 British Intelligence was not averse to assisting its new Soviet allies

---

1 Perhaps the disinclination to follow up Mason-MacFarlane's suggestion lay in a recognition of a somewhat fanciful element to his nature. In 1940 when Director of Military Intelligence with the British Expeditionary Force in France, Mason-MacFarlane advocated the kidnapping of British nationals who had been spreading defeatist rumours, stripping them of their clothes and abandoning them in the Bois de Bologne. Even one of his staff officers was moved to comment, 'I had to watch what I said because I always thought him quite capable of pulling a knife or a pistol on me' (Andrew 1985, p. 444).

in their plans to kill Hitler by bombing his headquarters. No. 30 Military Mission, the British liaison body in the Soviet Union, headed ironically by Mason-MacFarlane, was instructed to pass signals intelligence to the Russians. On 11 November 1941 it informed them (with Churchill's approval) 'that the Nazi leadership would be meeting at a "special train" at Orscha in Belorussia during inspections of the Eastern Front' (Smith 1996, p. 79). The next day the British confirmed the intelligence, adding that those present at the meeting would include all the senior German commanders on the Russian front. Although the area was bombed on the 13th by the Soviet Air Force, information was later received from the Russians that Hitler had not been present. In spite of this disappointment, the British continued to supply the Russians with details of the whereabouts of the German HQ which 'may have been helpful in pinpointing future Soviet efforts to eliminate the Nazi leadership through air raids' (ibid., p. 79).[1]

As the war progressed it was not just the Russians who tried to bomb Hitler, and increasingly members of the German Army discussed the possibilities of assassinating the war leader whose previous good fortune seemed to have deserted him. But if Hitler's series of strategic coups had been broken, his great personal luck was still in attendance. In February 1943 a group of officers determined to arrest or kill him when he visited their headquarters near Poltawa on the Eastern Front but, at the last moment, he flew to a different destination. A month later, an even more determined attempt was made. At Smolensk airfield on 7 March 1943, a bomb consisting of two British manufactured 'clam' charges disguised as bottles of brandy was handed to an unsuspecting member of Hitler's staff who then embarked upon Hitler's Focke-Wulfe Condor aircraft. Hitler was already on board and the aeroplane departed for the Führer's headquarters in East Prussia. The bomb should have detonated after half an hour's flight but two hours after take-off the conspirators were notified that the aircraft had landed safely at its destination. An officer was

---

1 The British had contemplated mounting an air raid to kill Hitler as early as July 1940 when D F Stevenson, the Director of Home Operations in the Air Ministry, had raised the question of RAF aircraft bombing the anticipated German victory parade in Paris. Stevenson was not, in fact, an advocate of the scheme and, as it transpired, the parade did not take place.

rushed to the headquarters at Rastenburg where the bomb was retrieved before it could be examined. It is believed that the very low temperature in the aircraft's storage compartment resulted in the detonator failing to set off the bomb's plastic explosive charge. A fortnight later another attempt was made, this time in the form of a suicide bomber. Armed with two bombs in the pockets of his greatcoat, Colonel von Gersdorff arranged to attend Hitler's visit to a Berlin Museum. He initiated one of the bomb's ten minute fuses and then tried to stay as close to Hitler as possible as he embarked upon his tour. But with his customary apparent sixth sense of self preservation, Hitler rushed through his visit and had left the building long before the fuse's time span. Fortunately, von Gersdorff was able to make his excuses and in a nearby lavatory extracted the fuse from the bomb. A similar method was planned by another officer at a display of new uniforms and equipment, this time using a grenade with only a $4^1/_2$ second fuse. But the would-be assassin was posted back to the Eastern Front before Hitler's inspection took place.

In contrast to the numerous attempts on Hitler's life and the extensive security arrangements surrounding him, Winston Churchill adopted a very low-key attitude to his personal safety. Shortly before the outbreak of war he felt that he was at risk from Nazi agents.

> I had at that time no official protection, and I did not wish to ask for any; but I though myself sufficiently prominent to take precautions. I had enough information to convince me that Hitler recognized me as a foe. My former Scotland Yard detective, Inspector Thompson, was in retirement. I told him to come along and bring his pistol with him. I got out my own weapons, which were good. While one slept, the other watched. Thus nobody would have had a walk-over.
>
> (Churchill 1948, p. 313)

In spite of his age and the fact that he had retired from the police in 1936 to run a grocer's shop, Thompson was a professional with a wealth of experience, having served as bodyguard to Lloyd George and then with Churchill throughout the 1920s. During the war he did not find the Prime Minister the easiest of men to protect, commenting that

Churchill during the Teheran conference, November/December 1943. His bodyguard, Detective Inspector Thompson, is on the extreme right
(IWM A 20739)

'Mr Churchill adopted his usual practice of ignoring advice he did not want to follow' (Thompson 1951, p. 95). In spite of this, Thompson, Scotland Yard's Special Branch and the armed forces were able to throw a highly effective security screen around the Prime Minister both in the United Kingdom and on his visits abroad. It was during one such foreign trip that perhaps the most serious threat to Churchill manifested itself. In November 1943 the 'Big Three' of Churchill, Roosevelt and Stalin met at Teheran to discuss the future conduct of the war. Soviet intelligence reported to their allies that they had learnt of a German assassination team in the area. Security was accordingly tightened, with the result that President Roosevelt moved from the vulnerable US Embassy and, when it was time to leave, Thompson used the Prime Minister's escorted convoy as a decoy and drove Churchill to the airfield in a nondescript army truck.

The Special Operations Executive

As has been seen, the British involvement in the various attempts on Hitler's life was restricted to SIGINT (signals intelligence) on the Eastern Front and the unintentional provision of British manufactured bombs that had been originally furnished for Resistance groups in Occupied Europe. The organization that had originally supplied these weapons was the Special Operations Executive (SOE). It had been created in July 1940 out of the War Office's MIR Department and SIS's Section D that had both begun to develop clandestine operations against Nazi Germany in 1938. MIR had tended to examine the future role of guerrilla warfare and paramilitary matters, whereas Section D was more concerned with 'dirty tricks', such as encouraging anti-Nazi movements abroad to engage in sabotage and subversion. The collapse of France in the summer of 1940 obliged the British government to consider the need for an organization that would foster resistance in the occupied countries. On 19 July 1940, Neville Chamberlain, in his new role as Lord President of the Council, announced in a memorandum to the War Cabinet that SOE would be formed under the auspices of the Ministry of Economic Warfare. Having been exhorted by Winston Churchill to 'Set Europe Ablaze', SOE's primary concern was to encourage and facilitate Resistance movements in occupied or enemy territory. It was difficult enough to develop effective action in countries under enemy subjugation but, after seven years of Nazi rule, Germany itself was considered almost impregnable. Consequently, only limited personnel and resources were allocated to SOE's German or 'X' Section. Some contacts were maintained with selected left-wing German opposition groups, largely by means of the Section's representatives in the neutral states on the borders of the Reich. In addition to these long-term political opponents of the Nazi regime, X Section was approached by dissident members of the German administration. In December 1942, elements within the German police force employed Dr Harry Söderman, a Swedish criminologist, to act as an intermediary with SOE. He brought news that the dissidents proposed to mount a coup in which they would arrest or execute all the leading Nazis. Fearing another SD provocation, the Foreign Office intervened and ordered SOE to break all contacts.

As specified in Chamberlain's memorandum, SOE was to be prepared from the outset to undertake 'all action by way of subversion and sabotage against the enemy overseas'. The brief did not exclude assassination, and one of SOE's first operations, in March 1941, was SAVANNA, a mission to ambush the aircrew of Kampfgeschwader 100 en route from their billets to their airfield near Vannes in Brittany. There had been initial opposition from Sir Charles Portal, the Chief of the Air Staff, who either did not approve of this ruthless approach to war or simply felt some sympathy with his fellow aviators in the Luftwaffe. He complained to a senior SOE staff officer:

> I think that the dropping of men dressed in civilian clothes for the purpose of attempting to kill members of the opposing forces is not an operation with which the Royal Air Force should be associated. I think you will agree that there is a vast difference, in ethics, between the time-honoured operation of the dropping of a spy from the air and this entirely new scheme for dropping what one can only call assassins.
>
> (Foot 1966, p. 153)

As it transpired, the Luftwaffe's travelling arrangements had altered by the time the team were parachuted and the operation was not completed.

There is no record whether later that year Portal's sensibilities received another buffeting when the RAF's No. 138 (Special Duty) Squadron dropped the ANTHROPOID team into Czechoslovakia to assassinate SS-Obergrüppenführer Reinhard Heydrich, the Acting Reich Protector of Bohemia and Moravia. The operation had been proposed by the Czechoslovaks, who requested SOE logistic and training facilities. Brigadier C McV Gubbins, SOE's Director of Operations, gave his approval, but elected not to inform Dr Hugh Dalton, the Minister of Economic Warfare, of his decision. SOE gave the two Czechoslovak soldiers intensive training at various SOE establishments in Scotland and England and parachuted them back to their homeland on 28/9 December 1941. Intelligence on Heydrich was limited and the assassins carried a vast array of weaponry in the hope of meeting every contingency. Their arsenal

Reinhard Heydrich
(IWM HU 47373)

*The remains of Heydrich's car after the assassination attempt
of 27 May 1942* (IWM HU 47379)

11

included handguns, a sub-machine gun, Mills bombs, anti-tank grenades, explosives, fuses, detonators, a spigot mortar and a lethal hypodermic syringe. Gubbins appears to have been less than optimistic of the agents' ability to carry out the attempt, and briefed Dalton's successor, Lord Selborne, to this effect. But against all the odds, on 27 May 1942, some six months after their arrival in the Protectorate, the assassins made their attack. Their approach was almost exactly in keeping with the instructions that they had received at the SOE Training School in Hertfordshire. One of the blast grenades was thrown against the side of Heydrich's car as it slowed at a hairpin corner on the outskirts of Prague. While not killed outright, their target was mortally wounded and died a week later of septicaemia. The assassins and a number of other agents sent from England were later betrayed and killed during a shoot-out in Prague with SS troops. The German reprisals resulted in the deaths of an estimated 5,000 civilians; this backlash soon became known in London, and SOE staff officers were left in no doubt over the potential ramifications of future assassination attempts on leading Nazis.

In spite of this, in the early spring of 1944, SOE mounted a co-ordinated assassination offensive, codenamed RATWEEK, aimed against the Nazi security forces across Occupied Europe. Resistance groups had frequently sought London's permission to liquidate collaborators, but RATWEEK marked a major development in SOE policy. The intention was to put the enemy on the back foot, creating confusion and trepidation at a time when the Allies were stepping up the preparations for the Resistance's important contribution to the Second Front. Full details of the campaign have not yet been released, but it is known that RATWEEK scored successes against Nazi personnel in Norway, Denmark, France and the Netherlands.

Operation Foxley

But was there ever any SOE initiative to attack the greatest target of all? It would appear that SOE had no significant plans to assassinate Adolf Hitler until 1944. In a letter of 20 June 1944 from Gubbins to General

Sir Hastings Ismay, Deputy Secretary (Military) to the War Cabinet, reference is made to a 1941 'project for eliminating Hitler that had received the approval of all Departments' (HS 6/623, p. 67). However no further details are given other than the intriguing comment that the operation was abandoned due to a sudden change in circumstances. The letter was in response to a telegram received the previous day from representatives in Algiers who reported that a source had come up with a 'project for killing Hitler' (HS 6/623, p. 69). Aware of the political ramifications, SOE's man in Algiers trod very carefully, referring the matter to his masters in London and liaising in North Africa with the Foreign Office. Not for the last time did such an ambitious scheme provoke concern that it would not be taken seriously, and the message concluded 'We are not repeat not mad nor is this a joke'. Gubbins, now a Major-General and SOE's Executive Head, wasted no time in asking for a ruling from the Chiefs of Staff advising him whether, if the information was confirmed, he should pursue the matter. The news from North Africa was not encouraging, with the Foreign Office revealing on 22 June that the 'reliable source' was a French Colonel who had 'reported that Hitler

Brigadier Colin Gubbins, SOE's *Director of Operations (centre), with Dr Hugh Dalton, the Minister of Economic Warfare (right), March 1941*
(IWM H 8185)

```
                                              — x'
                                              A/C⊃          62
                                              — AD/A-
                                              — MX'
                                                AD|H

TOP SECRET.


    PRIME MINISTER.
            I received a letter from S.O.E. this
    morning telling me that they had had information
    from Algiers of a project to kill Hitler, and
    asking whether the Chiefs of Staff agreed in
    principle to its immediate execution.   The
    Chiefs of Staff were unanimous that, from the
    strictly military point of view, it was almost
    an advantage that Hitler should remain in
    control of German strategy, having regard to
    the blunders that he has made, but that on the
    wider point of view, the sooner he was got out
    of the way the better.

    2.      Since then the telegram at Flag "A" has
    been received from Ambassador Duff Cooper.   I
    am told that, with your approval, the Foreign
    Secretary is instructing him to go ahead.
    Consequently the only object of this minute is
    to place on record that the Chiefs of Staff are
    in full agreement.

    3.      I have sent a copy of this minute to the
    Foreign Secretary.

                            (Signed)   H.L. ISMAY.


                            (Intld.)   W.S.C.
                                            22.6.

    21st June, 1944.
```

Ismay's minute to Churchill (PRO HS 6/623, p. 62)

was hiding in a chateau in Perpignan' (HS 6/623, p. 64). The proposal
was no longer that a *coup de main* operation be mounted by SOE, but
that the chateau be bombed from the air. SOE's involvement in the
project therefore ended. But the report had had the effect of making
SOE, the Chiefs of Staff, the Foreign Office and Churchill himself
address the fundamental question of whether they wished Hitler dead.
In his reply to Gubbins, Ismay sent a copy of a minute that he submitted
to the Prime Minister in which he outlined the Chiefs of Staff's position,
emphasising their low opinion of Hitler's generalship:

The Chiefs of Staff were unanimous that, from the strictly military point of view, it was almost an advantage that Hitler should remain in control of German strategy, having regard to the blunders that he has made, but that on the wider point of view, the sooner he was got out of the way the better.

(PRO HS 6/623, p. 62)

Gubbins certainly felt inspired to look at the matter more closely, encouraged by the intervention of a newcomer to SOE's ranks, Air Vice-Marshal A P Ritchie, the Air Adviser to the SOE Council (AD/A)[1] (PRO HS 6/623, p. 60). On 28 June most of the senior staff of SOE sat down to debate the matter. The brief minutes of the meeting record that Lieutenant-Colonel R H Thornley, the head of SOE's German Section, was strongly opposed to any plan to assassinate Hitler. However, it was apparent that he was in the minority and he had to content himself with advocating that if any operation were to be mounted, it should be disguised as an internal German matter in order to arouse maximum dissension within the enemy's ranks. Much to Thornley's chagrin, detailed planning for the operation, now codenamed FOXLEY, began.

SIS exhibited neither enthusiasm nor optimism regarding the project, but at a meeting on 1 July 1944 Major-General Sir Stewart Menzies, the Chief of the Secret Service, agreed to provide Gubbins with intelligence on Hitler's movements. A week later Air Commodore A P Boyle (A/CD) sent Gubbins a progress report confirming the contacts made with other departments and agencies but emphasising that the project was still very much in its infancy.

While FOXLEY gradually progressed, on 20 July 1944 the German resistance to Hitler mounted another assassination attempt of their own. A conspiracy of senior army officers, diplomats and politicians had joined in the most serious internal coalition against the Nazi regime. Although the figureheads of the plot included Field Marshals and Generals, a relatively junior officer, Colonel Claus von Stauffenberg,

---

1 Abbreviations in parentheses are symbols used in the documents.

The remains of the conference room at Rastenburg, East Prussia, after Stauffenberg's bomb. The arrow indicates where Hitler was standing at the time of the blast (IWM MH 211)

was the driving force behind the coup. He believed that its success was dependent upon eliminating as many as possible of the Nazi hierarchy at once, and decided to plant a bomb at one of the top-level briefings that he regularly attended. However, the opportunity to achieve this congregation of enemies did not materialize and, on 11 and 15 July, the bomb was not planted because neither Himmler nor Goering were present. Stauffenberg reluctantly changed his plans and decided to kill Hitler as soon as he got the opportunity. On 20 July he attended a conference at Hitler's headquarters in East Prussia and planted a bomb (manufactured from sabotage material dropped by SOE to the French Resistance) in the conference room. Making an excuse that he had to take a telephone call, he waited in a neighbouring hut until he heard the sound of an explosion. Convinced that no-one could have survived such a blast, he made his way to the airfield and flew to Berlin where he still had a vital role to play in the development of the coup.

16

But although the bomb had devastated the room, killing four and wounding all of the other 20 occupants, Hitler had survived. He suffered minor burns and abrasions, and the blast had perforated his eardrums, but he remained in command of his senses. Not without some justification he was heard to repeat 'I am invulnerable, I am immortal' (Hoffmann 1979, p. 252), but his salvation had a more prosaic explanation. Had the meeting been held in one of the complex's concrete bunkers, the blast would have been sufficient to kill those around the conference table. Similarly, if Stauffenberg had had the time to activate the second bomb in his briefcase, it is likely that Hitler would have been killed by the increased explosion.

In Berlin, even Stauffenberg's determination failed to galvanize his fellow conspirators as news began to emerge of Hitler's escape. The quick thinking of Goebbels and the loyalty of the commander of a key army unit swung the day and the coup was rapidly crushed. The ringleaders of the conspiracy were arrested and several, including Stauffenberg, were executed. Further arrests were followed by show trials and some 200 executions. Any hope of an effective anti-Nazi coup organized from within Germany was over.

SOE's reaction to the July Plot was rather detached. The coup's failure was seen in many ways as a vindication of the British policy of non-involvement with the German Resistance. Thornley in particular was scathing in his criticisms of the conspirators, implying somewhat erroneously in a letter to a fellow SOE officer that the whole plot had been infiltrated by Himmler. But Thornley could afford little time for gloating, with major changes afoot in SOE reflecting the new course the war had taken following the Allied landings. Arguably the most significant shift was in SOE's attitude towards operations into Germany. On 2 August 1944 Gubbins stated that 'Germany must now be the first priority target for SOE and all our energies and resources must be concentrated on the penetration of the Reich itself' (PRO HS 6/621). This was underlined by the establishment of a Committee on Germany upon which most of SOE's senior staff officers sat, and in October the creation of a German Directorate under Gubbins' old friend

Major-General G W R Templer. In spite of Gubbins' earlier exhortation, efforts against Germany were ultimately far from extensive (certainly when compared with SOE's contribution to the Resistance in Occupied Europe). Operations were in the event largely speculative, with a concentration upon Black Propaganda and the suborning and recruitment of German prisoners of war as potential agents (codenamed BONZOS). Another group, called PERIWIGS, consisted of Germans recruited as part of a deception scheme to lay false trails of a major Resistance movement in the Reich. Other schemes included counterfeiting German postage stamps picturing Himmler instead of Hitler, and the production of 'malingerer kits' for the German armed forces (HS 6/641, p. 86).

Meanwhile something of a hiatus had descended over the plan to kill Hitler; a hiatus that was only broken on 9 October 1944 by a memo from Thornley to Gubbins's senior staff officer Colonel R H Barry (CD/S). He reiterated his concerns over FOXLEY, and starkly concluded:

8. If this assassination is attempted, I adhere to my original view that it must be made to look as if the German Army was responsible.

9. The difficulties of this operation are obvious and, with the best will in the world, I do not think it can be achieved without being traceable to Allied sources.

10. In view of the above, it would not be in the interests of the Allied Cause for SOE to attempt the assassination of Hitler.

(PRO HS 6/623, p. 54)

Unfortunately for Thornley, Ritchie was still proving to be a major advocate of FOXLEY, and as the former was penning his critical memorandum, the latter was writing one of his own urging the plan's continuation. Ritchie got his way and it was agreed by the SOE Council on 10 October to continue preparations for FOXLEY. It was an unhappy position for Thornley, ostensibly SOE's expert on Germany, to have his opinions disregarded in favour of a staff officer with little depth of knowledge. But there was no stopping FOXLEY's impetus, and on 8 November Thornley (confusingly using the AD/X symbol as the originator) instructed the head of the German Directorate's planning staff to produce 'a final paper' on the subject, while warning of the 'grave divergence of views'. Although he conceded 'among certain Members of the Council and among the highest in the land in England, there are strong advocators of FOXLEY I' (HS 6/623, p. 47), he could not resist stating that 'all experts on Germany with whom I have been able to discuss FOXLEY I are in agreement with me that it is unsound and would not be in the interests of the Allied Cause.' He also mentioned the not irrelevant consideration that 'as yet, no candidate has been found to attempt this difficult task'. In spite of this evident divergence of opinion at the centre of SOE, intelligence reports continued to arrive, helping to build up a picture of the potential target. Interrogations of German prisoners of war proved particularly useful, and SIGINT reports, described as 'a most secret and sure source' (HS 6/623, p. 40), gave details of the location of Hitler's headquarters.

The plan

The SOE plan to assassinate Adolf Hitler outlined in Operation FOXLEY (PRO HS 6/624; reproduced in full here, pp. 35–158) is essentially a briefing document outlining the intelligence available to SOE's planners and seeking to develop, but in no major detail, the most likely *modus operandi*. There is no specific attribution of its authorship, but indications among the supporting documents suggest that it was written by an intelligence officer, Major H B Court (L/BX). It appears to have been largely drawn up from open sources available before the war – detailed interrogations of German prisoners of war,[1] and to a lesser extent intelligence obtained from enemy wireless traffic. The latter is not as evident as might have been expected given the British Government Code and Cipher School's successes against enciphered German signals. The documents suggest that Hitler's presence would have been indicated to the assassination team by a flag flown over his residence, the arrival

---

1 One photograph on the file shows Hitler receiving King Boris of Bulgaria, with the informant indicated among the guard of honour.

The interior of Hitler's study in the Berghof with its commanding views of the Obgersalzberg (IWM HU 63538)

of his train or the appearance of his bodyguard in local hostelries. It might have been anticipated that SIGINT would have provided more substantial assistance. Much of the information in the report is avowedly out of date, and a great deal relates to conditions prevailing before the war. The most contemporary body of knowledge is cited as being current in April/May 1944, although a footnote (5; p. 38 this volume) mentions Hitler's whereabouts on 3 August.

The primary location under examination is the area around the town of Berchtesgaden in Southern Bavaria. Here on the Obersalzberg, Hitler built the Berghof, an alpine retreat that grew into a major, formal residence that in turn resulted in the development of support services, barracks and the construction of chalets for other members of the Nazi hierarchy. The details given of the topography and the layout of buildings making up the complex are clearly the type of information essential in the planning of an assassination, but the material on perimeter fences, patrols and sentries could only be used as general guidelines prior to a local investigation by the team chosen to carry out the job.

A British soldier examines a PIAT anti-tank weapon
(IWM B 14328)

The plan for assassinating Hitler at the Berghof basically breaks down into three options. The first would consist of one or two snipers, disguised in German Gebirgsjäger uniforms, who would lie in wait for Hitler on his daily walk to the teahouse where he customarily took breakfast. If the attempt (using explosive bullets) failed, it was suggested that a back-up team armed with the British PIAT (Projectile Infantry Anti-Tank) or American Bazooka might fire an explosive charge at the teahouse in which Hitler had taken sanctuary. The second option was the ambushing of Hitler's motor convoy as it left the Berghof. The PIAT or Bazooka was to be employed, but in order to have a chance of hitting the target, the attack would have to be launched when the car was being driven slowly at a sharp bend. The third and most fanciful of the options was a parachute drop of a battalion of the Special Air Service (SAS) under cover of an air raid. Rather optimistically the report suggests that 'A paratroop battalion could therefore swamp any resistance of the troops guarding the OBERSALZBERG might put up' (76; p. 113 this volume). Bearing in mind the constant uncertainty over Hitler's whereabouts, the unconfirmed strength of the German garrison, the vagaries of the weather (the right conditions being vital to a bombing raid and a parachute drop) and the absence of any consideration of the force's exfiltration from Bavaria, it is hard to contemplate this option being adopted.

A considerable amount of information had also been gathered about Hitler's private railway train, and opportunities were examined for attacking him while he boarded the train or while it was in motion. One of the German prisoner of war informants had been a steward on von Ribbentrop's train, and some rather hopeful assumptions were made by the planners that the configuration of the Foreign Minister's would be the same as that of the Führer. Details of the security arrangements for when Hitler's train stopped at stations seem particularly vague: 'This information, it is true, dates from 1940, when Hitler was in his heyday, and it is possible that safety measures have been tightened up of late' (93; p. 130 this volume).

Perhaps the most practical option that was proposed against the train was having a sniper or PIAT firing at Hitler as he embarked. But the writer of the report had a very optimistic appreciation of the capabilities of the weaponry, commenting that a 300-yard shot would be 'probably within range of a PIAT gun' (97; p. 134 this volume). Most other sources suggest that it was only effective up to 100 yards.

Interestingly, there seems to have been little prospect of introducing a bomb on the train. The report contains the intriguing statement that 'Interference with the drinking and cooking water is the only clandestine means which offers itself' (99; p. 136 this volume). By recruiting foreign workers who cleaned the exterior of the train, it was hoped to introduce a 'suitable medium' (a euphemism for poison) into the train's kitchen water supply. It was gauged that 768 grammes of the poison would be sufficient to create a lethal strength in the 540 litre tank. The 'medium' 'I' was chosen in preference to 'R' and 'F' because the victims would not suffer symptoms until after almost a week. Even when they did succumb, the report was able to claim that 'under such circumstances there is no antidote'. In the knowledge of Hitler's unusual diet, it was anticipated that the best chance of his ingesting the poison would be in coffee or tea.

Hitler salutes an admiring crowd from his train, April 1941 (IWM)

It is surprising that in the light of SOE's extensive experience of railway sabotage the plans to derail Hitler's train are among the weakest aspects of the FOXLEY plans. Great store is set by an account of an attempted derailment carried out by Polish saboteurs in the autumn of 1941. The report claims that by chance Hitler's train ceded priority to another, with the result that 430 Germans were killed in a derailment intended for their Führer. Unfortunately the account failed to make the writer realize that the sabotage of a particular train requires specific and advance information – commodities in short supply in the FOXLEY reports. Warnings would only be possible with the complicity of railway workers, and in the absence of this assistance the laying of explosive charges on the line would be merely speculative. The nadir of the railway schemes was reached with the suggestion that an agent wait on a station platform for Hitler's train to pass. At the crucial moment the saboteur would fling a suitcase filled with explosives under the wheels of the train. The writer of the report points out that 'For this the train would have to be passing on a track adjacent to the platform on which the operative was standing or only one track removed therefrom, and the operator be prepared to take the consequences' (104; p. 140 this volume). It is uncertain whether the writer's concern over the agent's ability to throw a suitcase full of explosives across one or two tracks blinded him to the matter of how the explosives would be detonated.

Only passing consideration is given to the agents who might have carried out FOXLEY. In the introduction, the author suggests 'Austrian or Bavarian Ps/W with an animus against the Nazis (and Hitler in particular); Poles or Czechs' (5; p. 38 this volume). It is conceded that they would require training in the United Kingdom or at one of SOE's other training centres and that they would need to be parachuted near Salzburg or infiltrated by land. It may be reasonably assumed that the German and Austrian Jews who had taken refuge in Britain before the war and had volunteered for service with SOE would have had sufficient 'animus against the Nazis', but they do not appear to have been considered for the operation. An officer who may have been in line for the task, or at least one aspect of it, was Captain E H Bennett. An exchange of telegrams between London and New York reveal that he was being 'considered for a high priority assassination task which would require his lying low in Germany for a considerable period collecting necessary intelligence to enable him to do the job' (HS 6/623, p. 7). But on 26 March 1945 London signalled that it would not require Bennett's services after all.

Foxley II

Hitler was not the only potential target for assassination that SOE considered. As early as 8 July 1944 Air Commodore Boyle recommended that Heinrich Himmler might join his leader as suitable for elimination (PRO HS 6/623, p. 56). This expansion of the project was given the title FOXLEY II, and on 8 November 1944 even Thornley concurred, stating it was 'an operation which will have everyone's backing and which should be very carefully studied' (HS 6/623, p. 48).

To: C.D.   **TOP SECRET**   ACD/79B/5775

From: A/CD   8th July, 1944.

Copies to: X and L/BX.

C.D.
9 JUL 1944
4

56

ACTION.....................................

Operation FOXLEY.   COPIES TO.....................

CIRCULATE TO.....C₂/I/-/-/ v/₀ -c₀

1. I give below brief details of progress made. G+

2. Contacts.

   (a) C. has given instructions that every item of
       information regarding Hitler's movements, well-
       being, habits, etc., is to be sent to me, via
       V.C.S.S., at once.

   (b) War office contact has been intensified, and use-
       ful information received (see below).

   (c) Air Ministry have been asked to make detailed
       survey of use of aircraft by Hitler.

   (d) P.I.D. (Sefton Delmer) has been instructed to co-operate
       with L/BX.

3. Information.

   (a) Location of Headquarters of Hitler at Schloss
       KLESSHEIM, 47° 49' N., 12° 58' E., have been
       established.

   (b) Useful reports (delayed in some cases) regarding
       movements in France, have been received.

   (c) Details of personal guards, flak, etc., are being
       prepared.

   (d) Collated reports on personal habits of Hitler
       being prepared from P/W interrogations and C.S.D.I.C.
       reports.

   (e) Photographic reconnaissance of frequented places
       being requested.

4. FOXLEY II.?

   It has been suggested (and I seek direction on the point)
   that it will be advisable to couple Himmler with Hitler
   in the contemplated operation. Indeed, the abolition of
   Himmler would, in many respects, be more advantageous for
   reasons into which I need not go, and preparation of the
   necessary intelligence regarding the pair will be no more
   difficult than for individual treatment.

5. Plans.

   It is too early to give any outline of plans for the attempt
   but the following gives a rough outline which will be
   developed as soon as possible, though I emphasize that,
   as we are working more or less from scratch and have no
   real contacts with foreign workers in Germany, we must not
   expect results of any sort speedily or at all.

   (a) The collection and collation of information must
       continue every day. There are many untapped sources.

   (b) Choice and assembly of a team of assassins. No easy

*The first page of Air Commodore Boyle's memo recommending
Himmler's assassination* (PRO HS 6/623, p. 56)

P/T.1/98.   *Top secret*   18th December, 1944.

TO: AD/X.   FROM: X/PLANS.   33

1.   Has the possibility of using HESS for Foxley II ever been considered?

2.   HESS might either be bluffed into doing it with the reason given to him that it might open a way for peace negotiations or, alternatively, be hypnotised into doing it.

3.   HESS is known to be an extremely nervous individual and should be very susceptible to hypnotic treatment.

4.   Has hypnotism ever been considered by us for our operations?

5.   You are most probably aware of the success which an American Officer stationed in Ireland claims in this field?

                                              X/PLANS.

Manderstam's memo suggesting that Hess be hynotized
into eliminating Himmler (PRO HS 6/623, p. 33)

Rudolph Hess
(IWM MH 7430)

Heinrich Himmler
(IWM PIC 65669)

But then FOXLEY II lurched into fantasy. On 18 December 1944 Major L H Manderstam (X/PLANS) submitted one of the most bizarre SOE memoranda ever written, enquiring whether 'the possibility of using HESS for Foxley II had ever been considered?' (PRO HS 6/623 p. 33) Hitler's former Deputy had flown to Britain in May 1941 in the hope of securing a negotiated peace, and, not unnaturally, his mental stability had been questioned by both his British captors and his erstwhile Nazi comrades. He therefore seemed the least suitable of candidates to undertake the assassination of Himmler even if, as Manderstam suggested, he might be 'bluffed' or 'hypnotised' into undertaking the task. Incredibly, Templer approved a request for access to intelligence material on Hess, but the file reveals that on 8 January 1945 Manderstam had to submit a questionnaire regarding Hess, and it might be deduced that access to the files had been denied him. Meanwhile, Major H B Court, an intelligence officer on SOE's staff, brought some sense back into the proceedings by suggesting SS Officers who might be added to the list of FOXLEY II targets. A further ray of common sense was invoked by Captain J B Joll on 22 February 1945 when he stated that 'It seems unlikely at the present state of the war that we shall obtain sufficient up-to-date intelligence to plan a specific FOXLEY operation against HIMMLER or any other Party leader or prominent SD official' (PRO HS 6/623, p. 9).

In spite of Joll's pessimism, Court produced a detailed summary of four leading candidates as targets for FOXLEY II. At the top of the list was Josef Goebbels, the Minister of Propaganda, Gauleiter of Berlin and Reich Plenipotentiary for Total War. Joining him were SS-Obersturmbannführer Otto Skorzeny, the leading German proponent of special operations, and two officers who had close connections with Goebbels, Generalmajor Otto Remer and Generalleutnant Bruno von Hauenschild. Although the report carried detailed summaries of Goebbels's duties, habits and likely whereabouts and Skorzeny's service career and current postings, they scarcely provided sufficient intelligence to mount an assassination operation. The two army officers appear to have been included because their proximity to Goebbels might have made them secondary targets in a mission to kill

27

him. Joll's verdict seems to sum up the generally lukewarm attitude to both FOXLEY and FOXLEY II felt by the more perspicacious of SOE's staff officers:

> I have studied the attached and feel that GOEBBELS is the only target on which we have enough intelligence to attempt to mount an operation. I feel it might be worth considering if you have any suitable Bonzos, though I am afraid any intelligence on BERLIN will probably be out of date by the time such an operation could be mounted.
>
> (PRO HS 6/626, p. 2)

By the beginning of April 1945 FOXLEY II had been overtaken by events. Boyle wrote a memorandum to Gubbins that the time for attempting to disorganize the German intelligence service was past and that SOE should be more concerned with arresting German Intelligence officers than engaging in 'a certain thinning of the ranks of the RSHA'[1] (HS 6/623, pp. 3–4).

Conclusion

With the benefit of hindsight, Operation FOXLEY offers an unusual insight into British attitudes towards the Nazi regime in the closing years of the war. With the exception of Portal, no-one in Whitehall seems to have even begun to question the ethics of assassination. The sole considerations appear to have been whether the operation was feasible and, if so, whether its implementation would achieve the desired result in weakening the German war effort. The answer to both is an emphatic 'no'. The plan demanded a specialist team, but as Hitler himself commented:

> not a soul could cope with an assassin who, for idealistic reasons, was prepared quite ruthlessly to hazard his own life in the

---

1 Reichssicherheitshauptamt, the central body coordinating the work of the German security and intelligence organizations.

Joseph Goebbels with his detectives (PRO HS 6/626, p. 6)

Otto Skorzeny
(PRO HS 6/626, p. 25)

29

execution of his object. I quite understand why 90 per cent of the historic assassinations have been successful.

(Hitler 1953, p. 366)

In spite of the apparently impressive collation of data in the files, the intelligence seems insufficient to have justified the launching of an attempt. An SOE assassination team bearing an arsenal of weaponry could not have travelled around Germany looking for their quarry in the way Bavaud had done, especially with the prevailing wartime conditions of bombing, dislocation of travel and rigorous security checks. The fundamental problem of keeping track of Hitler's whereabouts was never adequately solved, and planning for an attack at the Berghof continued in blissful ignorance of the fact that Hitler left Berchtesgaden on 14 July 1944 never to return.

It was therefore just as well that SOE's superiors were not forcing them to undertake a mission that was so fundamentally flawed. Far from it. While FOXLEY's advocates lay within SOE's own ranks, from Churchill downwards there existed a widespread conviction that the elimination of Hitler would not be advantageous and may be positively counter-productive. John Wheeler-Bennett, an adviser on German affairs to the Foreign Office, predicted that the elimination of Hitler would prove detrimental to Allied strategy. He wrote to Anthony Eden, the Foreign Secretary, on 25 July 1944, shortly after the Bomb Plot, 'It may now be said with some definiteness that we are better off with things as they are today than if the plot of July 20th had succeeded and Hitler had been assassinated' (Gilbert 1986, p. 868). Wheeler-Bennett felt that the success of the conservative military conspiracy may have raised the prospect of surrender terms other than the unconditional demands agreed by the Allies. In a distinctly cold blooded statement he argued that 'the present purge [on the July Plot conspirators] is presumably removing from the scene numerous individuals who might have caused us difficulty, not only had the plot succeeded, but also after the defeat of a Nazi Germany' (ibid.).

But, appropriately, it was Churchill who provided a proper perspective on the question of assassination attempts against Hitler. He

Comments on Operation Foxley by SOE *staff officers*
(PRO HS 6/625, p. 15)

remained convinced that Hitler and Nazi Germany needed to be beaten on the battlefield rather than trusting in the accuracy of a sniper's bullet. In a speech to the House of Commons on 2 August 1944, he said: 'decisive as they [attempts on Hitler's life] may be one of these days, it is not in them that we should put our trust, but in our own strong arms and the justice of our cause' (ibid.).

Select Bibliography

Andrew, C (1985) *Secret Service* (London: Heinemann).

Churchill, W (1948) *The Second World War. Volume 1: The Gathering Storm* (London: Cassell).

Cantwell, J D (1998) *The Second World War: A Guide to Documents in the Public Record Office* (Richmond, Surrey: PRO).

Foot, M R D (1966) SOE *in France* (London: HMSO).

Gilbert, M (1986) *Road to Victory* (London: Heinemann).

Hitler, A (1953) *Hitler's Secret Conversations, 1941–1944* (New York: Farrar, Straus & Young).

Hoffman, P (1977) *The History of the German Resistance 1933–1945* (London: Macdonald and Jane's).

Hoffman, P (1979) *Hitler's Personal Security* (London: Macmillan).

Höhne, H (1969) *The Order of the Death's Head* (London: Secker & Warburg).

MacDonald, C (1989) *The Killing of SS Obergruppenführer Reinhard Heydrich* (London: Macmillan).

Mason, H M (1979) *To Kill Hitler* (London: Michael Joseph).

Smith, B F (1996) *Sharing Secrets with Stalin* (Lawrence: University Press of Kansas.

Tennant, P (1992) *Touchlines of War* (Hull: University of Hull Press).

Thompson, W H (1951) *I was Churchill's Shadow* (London: Christopher Johnson).

Wilkinson, P and Bright Astley, J (1993) *Gubbins and* SOE (London: Leo Cooper).

The Documents

Operation
FOXLEY. TOP SECRET

Contents.

Operation.
FOXLEY.

INTRODUCTION.

1. Object: The elimination of HITLER and any high-ranking
              Nazis or members of the Führer's entourage
              who may be present at the attempt.

2. Means: Sniper's rifle, PIAT gun (with graze fuze) or
              Bazooka, H.E. and splinter grenades; derailment
              and destruction of the Führerzug by explosives;
              clandestine means.

3. Scene of   The most recent information available on Hitler
operations: and his movements narrows down the field of
              endeavour to two loci of action, viz. the
              BERCHTESGADEN area and the Führerzug (Hitler's
              train).

              The BERCHTESGADEN area includes the OBER-
              SALZBERG as well as the road from the BERGHOF
              (Hitler's residence on the OBERSALZBERG) to
              SCHLOSS KLESSHEIM, one of the alternative
              Führerhauptquartiers which were set up in
              Germany following the threat to the RASTENBURG
              (East Prussia) FHQ by the advance of the Russian
              armies in Poland.

              Loci of action in connection with the
              Führerzug include the SCHLOSS KLESSHEIM sidings,
              SALZBURG railway station and the routes followed
              by Hitler's train when travelling north (to
              Berlin) and west (to Mannheim).

4. Operatives: Austrian or Bavarian Ps/W with an animus
              against the Nazis (and Hitler in particular);
              Poles or Czechs (in view of the large number
              of foreign workers of these nationalities in
              the Berchtesgaden - Salzburg district).
              Operatives might be trained in this country
              or abroad (e.g. Italy or Slovenia), and dropped
              over or infiltrated into enemy territory in the
              vicinity of Salzburg, where if necessary they
              could make contact with and receive assistance
              from anti-Nazi friends and relations (Austrians
              and Bavarians) or from foreign workers (Poles
              and Czechs).

5. Planning   Whereas it might be possible to plan and execute
              the operations described in Part I - Berchtes-
              gaden area - "from the book", a final check-up
              of conditions in the Salzburg area and/or on
              the Führerzug's routes would be advised before
              drawing up the final plan of action. This, it
              is suggested, should be made on the spot by the
              operatives (or their leader) entrusted with the
              execution of the project.

+ Though Hitler, it is quite definite, was there on 3rd August,
   if not later.

38

Part I. THE BERCHTESGADEN AREA AS THE SCENE OF ACTION.

A. Climate and Topography.

1. Climate. The climate of BERCHTESGADEN is in general
colder in winter and hotter in summer and autumn
than in England.

The chief characteristic of the weather is that
it is fairly stable. When it rains, it usually goes
on for several days or weeks - similarly in the case
of snow. There was on one occasion last winter 14
days' downfall of snow. When it is fine it usually
stays fine for several days.

Snow falls fairly early because of the altitude,
sometimes as early as September. In 1943 snow fell
in November, but there was a long spell of fine
weather around Christmas.

Fog is very rare, and normally occurs either in
the valley, coming no higher than the GUTSHOF, or
the heights surrounding the KEHLSTEIN. It is very
rare that the BERGHOF and the SS barracks are wrapped
in fog. The weather month by month in the period
August 1943 - May 1944 was as follows:-

Aug.	1943.	Very fine; rain only on two or three days.
Sept.	" .	Very fine and still very warm up to middle of month when it became wet.
Oct.	" .	Sky overcast with constant downpours of rain and sleet. Some snow already began to fall.
Nov.	" .	Rainy. Occasional snow which did not stay on the ground.
Dec.	" .	On 20 Dec. snow began to fall (lasting two weeks). This type of weather went on throughout the winter.
Jan.	1944.	Maximum depth of snow in the OBER-SALZBERG was 2 metres - on the ROSS-FELD 4 metres and 6-8 metres on the WATZMANN.
Feb.	" .	The downfall of snow slackened and by the middle of the month the FÜHRERSTRASSE was clear of snow.
March.	" .	Still a few days of snow but weather on the whole fine.
April.	" .	Occasional snow. Otherwise typical April weather.
May.	" .	This type of weather continued into May when it was still possible to ski.

2. General notes on the topography of the area. (see
Sketch Map - Fig.1.). OBERSALZBERG lies in an
amphitheatre of the Bavarian Alps adjacent to the
former Austrian frontier. The dominating peaks and
ranges are, in the north-west the UNTERSBERG (1973m.),
in the south-west the LATTENGEBIRGE and WATZMANN
peaks, in the south the HOHER GÖLL (2522m.) and in
the east the ROSSFELD ridge (1608m.).

Also shown in colour pp. 160–61

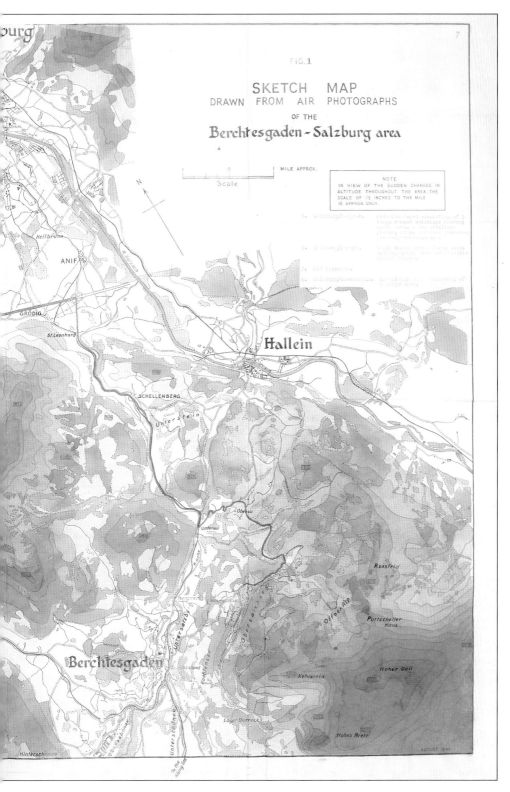

FIG.1

SKETCH MAP
DRAWN FROM AIR PHOTOGRAPHS

OF THE

Berchtesgaden - Salzburg area

MILE APPROX.

Scale

NOTE
IN VIEW OF THE SUDDEN CHANGES IN
ALTITUDE THROUGHOUT THE AREA, THE
SCALE OF 1½ INCHES TO THE MILE
IS APPROX ONLY.

AUGUST 1944

Here the bare limestone peaks and glacier-
scaped slopes of the Alps give way to a jumble
of pine-clad foothills, interspersed with wide
stretches of open grass- and meadowland.

The BAD REICHENHALL-BERCHTESGADEN-HALLEIN
area is drained in the east by the SALZACH, in the
west by the SAALACH and in the centre by the ACHE
which, on leaving the NONNTAL defile (the route
taken by HITLER when travelling from the OBERSALZBERG
to SCHLOSS KLESSHEIM) enters the SALZBURG plain near
St. LEONHARD to flow into the SALACH south of ANIF.

The greater part of the OBERSALZBERG as well
as the road from the BERGHOF as far as GRÖDIG (on
the way to SCHLOSS KLESSHEIM) is very hilly and
densely wooded and should therefore afford good
cover, even in winter, as most of the trees are of
the non-deciduous variety.

Since the route taken to SCHLOSS KLESSHEIM
makes use of the Autobahn which skirts the MAXGLAN
suburb of SALZBURG the attempt would have to be
made from the woods between the OBERSALZBERG and
GRÖDIG or in the vicinity of the teahouse on the
MOOSLANER KOPF.

3. **Topography of the OBERSALZBERG** (see Fig.2).

(a) **General.** The entire area of the OBERSALZBERG
is for the most part very heavily wooded and, being
also extremely hilly, is a difficult area to guard.
This is also true of the area immediately around
HITLER's residence - the BERGHOF - which is known
as the FÜHRERGEBIET. In addition to BORMANN's and
GÖRING's residences, the guest houses, the quarters
of HITLER's personal and domestic staffs, the SS
barracks, the PLATTERHOF - once an hotel-de-luxe
and now a hospital - and the hutments of foreign
(Czech) workmen, etc., the FÜHRERGEBIET also includes
the KEHLSTEIN (or KEHLSTEINGEBIET). The KEHLSTEIN
is approached by a zig-zag road (see Fig.1). which
however becomes so steep towards the summit that
lifts, one for passengers and the other for vehicles,
have been installed for the last 300 feet to the
Teahouse, a stone building frequently visited by
HITLER at one time. Nearby is a wooden hut and in
the vicinity a house, hidden away, belonging to
BORMANN, in which HITLER is said to have 'lain
low' in 1923.

The woods
    in the vicinity of the RODELBAHN;
    behind the MOOSLANER KOPF; (near the Teehaus
        visited by HITLER on his morning walks);
    north of the BERGHOF; and
    round the KEHLSTEIN
are particularly thick.

Except above the 1400 metre line on the KEHL-
STEIN, which is a very tricky area to climb, the
entire FÜHRERGEBIET is passable on foot. In winter
the lower slopes of the KEHLSTEIN are passable on
skis, and a very good skier could negotiate the
slopes of the RODELBAHN. Skiing on the FÜHRERSTRASSE
in the vicinity of the BERGHOF is forbidden.

Fig.2. Key-map of the OBERSALZBERG from air photos.

1. The Berghof.
2. Haus Türken.
3. Gästehaus Hoher Göll.
4. Holtzplatz.
5. Platterhof.
6. Gefolgschafthaus.
7. SS barracks.
8. Vordereck.
9. Modellbau and Kindergarten.
10. Spahn Häusl.
11. Haus Bormann.
12. Landhaus Göring.
13. Büchenhöhe.
14. Staatliche Bauleitung.
15. Lager Riemenfeld.
16. Klaushöhe.
17. Hintereck.

18. Adjutantur Göring.
19. Gärtnerei.
20. Post.
21. Kampfhäusl.
22. Jugendverpflegungsheim and Maierhaus.
23. Theaterhalle, Obersalzberg.
24. Lager Antenberg.
25a. Berghäusl.
25b. Haus Speer.
25c. Meisterlehen.
25d. Berghang.
26. Atelier Speer.
27. Baumgartlehen.
28. Gutshof Obersalzberg.
29. Beckstein Haus.
30. Teehaus (Mooslaner Kopf).
31. Bienenhaus.

Tracks.

Roads (vehicles).

Führerstrasse.

Wire fences. (Position of wire fences is only approximate, since they have been sketched from memory).

SS patrols.

SS piquets.

Civilian piquets, i.e. Posten Berghof, Antenberg, Teugelbrunn, Rosenbahn, Auerstrasse.

Woods (pines and other non-deciduous trees).

Undergrowth, scrub and deciduous trees.

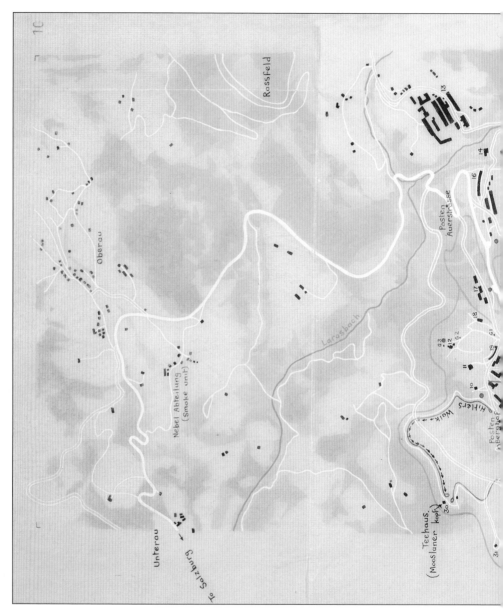

Also shown in colour pp. 162–3

44

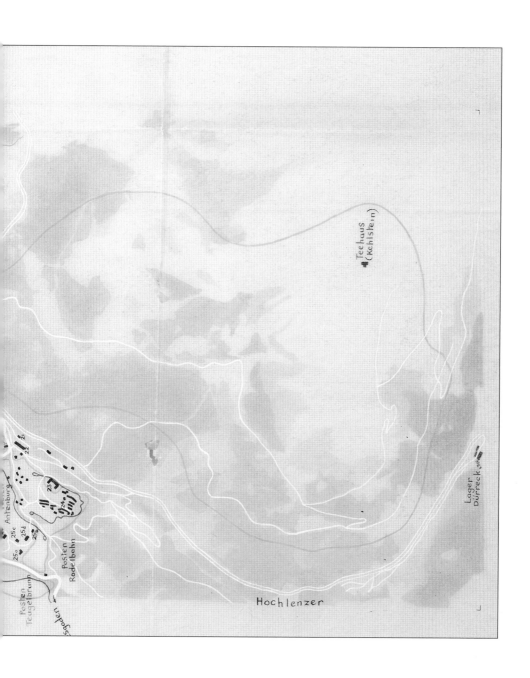

Teehaus (Kehlstein)

Lager Dürreck

Hochlenzer

Posten Rodelbahn

Posten Teugelbrunn

Antenburg

45

All roads are kept clear of snow in winter.
In summer only a few patches of snow remain on the
KEHLSTEIN (1834m.).

(b) Layout of the buildings on the OBERSALZBERG.
The various buildings in and around the FÜHRERGEBIET
are shown in Fig.2. They include:-

(1) The BERGHOF. Formerly a chalet with stone
ground floor and wooden upper floor known as the
HAUS WACHENFELD (Figs.3a-3d), this building has
been considerably extended since HITLER acquired it
as his country residence in the early 1920s. Figs.
4a, 4b and 5 give an idea of the modifications
which have since been made to it. Fig.6 gives a
plan of the ground floor of the building (as in
April/May 1944). In addition to part of the Begleitkommando (HITLER's escort) it also houses one of
the three telephone exchanges on the OBERSALZBERG.

(2) HAUS TÜRKEN. Formerly the Hotel (Pension)
ZUM TÜRKEN this building provides sleeping quarters
for the piquets of the SS Wachkompanie OBERSALZBERG,
the SS guardroom and accommodation for the security
personnel (Reichsicherheitsdienst) of the OBERSALZ-
BERG. Another telephone exchange is installed here
which is operated by personnel of the SS-Kommando
OBERSALZBERG. Fig.7 gives plan, side and front
elevations of the Haus Türken.

(3) GÄSTEHAUS HOHER GÖLL. This guest house
lies in the woods back of the BERGHOF in the direction
of the KEHLSTEIN. It accommodates Frl. Eva (Evi)
BRAUN, Hitler's secretary and Press Chief Dr.
DIETRICH on his visits to the BERGHOF as well as
Hitler's aides-de-camp and less important guests.
It also houses RSD (security) personnel, including
Brigadeführer RATTENHUBER, who is in command of the
RSD at OBERSALZBERG. The guest house is run by a
Frl. JOSEPHA GUGGENBICHLER, who is the "Spiessin"
(supervisor) of the women in the district. There
is a teleprinter installation in the building which
is operated by men of the Führerbegleitbataillon
(Hitler's escort battalion) from the Grossdeutschland
Division. This unit normally provides the guard at
FHQ/OKW. Fig.8 gives plan, side and front elevations
of the Gästehaus (see also Fig.11).

(4) HOLZPLATZ. This is a sawmill (wooden hut)
with a motor-driven saw worked by a German employee
who lives on the KLAUSHÖHE.

(5) PLATTERHOF. Designed as an hotel-de-luxe
and only completed in 1942, the Platterhof (Fig.9)
is now a hospital for severely wounded members of
the Wehrmacht. It houses some 80-100 patients.
The coiffeur in charge of the barber's shop under
the hospital (Fig.10) speaks fluent Italian (and
German with a Bavarian accent); he employs three
Italian assistants.

The Bergschenke (Fig.9) consists of a Bierstube
and restaurant with kitchen underneath. Five or six
waitresses (wearing blue "Dirndl" dresses) are
employed. They live in the GEFOLGESCHAFTHAUS.

Fig. 3a.

Fig. 3b.

Figs. 3a and 3b. Haus Wachenfeld in the 1920s prior to the
extensions preceding its transformation into the Berghof.
Note: The gateway in Fig. 3a has long since been removed to the
Posten Berghof (see Fig.2). The mountain in the background of
Fig. 3b is the WATZMANN.

Fig. 3c.

Fig. 3d.

Figs. 3c and 3d showing respectively views of the Haus
Wachenfeld from the opposite side to that in Fig. 3b, and of
the terrace (Fig. 3d).
Note: The mountains in the background of Fig. 3d are those of
the UNTERSBERG (see also view in Fig. 11 taken in the same
                         direction).

Fig. 4a.   The Berghof in early summer (Kehlstein in the
           background).
Note: Servants' quarters (right) and flagpole (left).

Fig. 4b.   The Berghof in winter (Kehlstein in the background).

The photograph in Fig. 4b was taken later than that in Fig. 4a
       and shows telephone exchange extension (left).

Hitler's bedroom is on the first floor (left-hand and centre
       window).

Fig. 5. The Berghof at a later date. This photograph was
taken from more or less the same direction as that in Fig. 3.

Note: Gate is no longer as shown in Fig. 3a (having been
       removed to Posten Berghof (see Fig. 2).
       The extension in the foreground houses the telephone
       exchange.

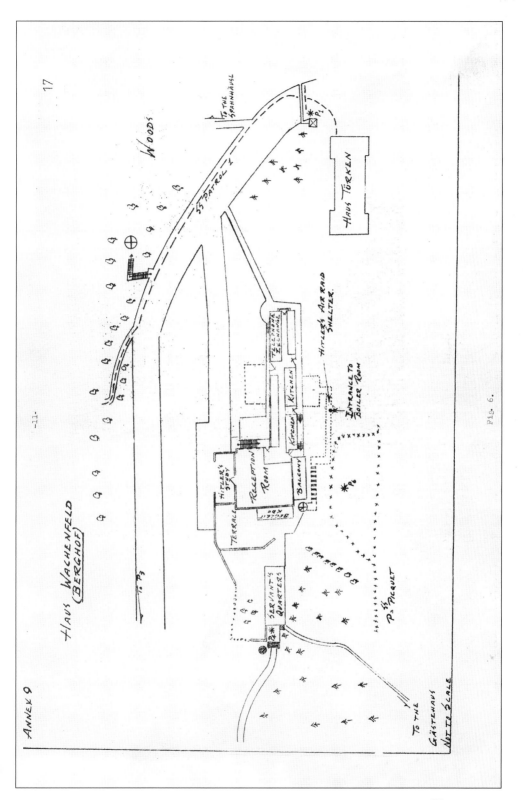

ANNEX 9

HAUS WACHENFELD (BERGHOF)

WOODS

TO THE SPAHNHÄUSL

HAUS TÜRKEN

SS PATROL 1

HITLER'S AIR RAID SHELTER.

ENTRANCE TO BOILER ROOM

HITLER'S STUDY

RECEPTION ROOM

KITCHEN

KITCHEN

TELEPHONE EXCHANGE

TERRACE

BALCONY

SERVANT'S QUARTERS

SS PICKET

TO THE GÄSTEHAUS

NOT TO SCALE

TO P₃

Fig. 6.

ANNEX 8

-12-

18

HAUS TÜRKEN

Front view
(Not to scale)

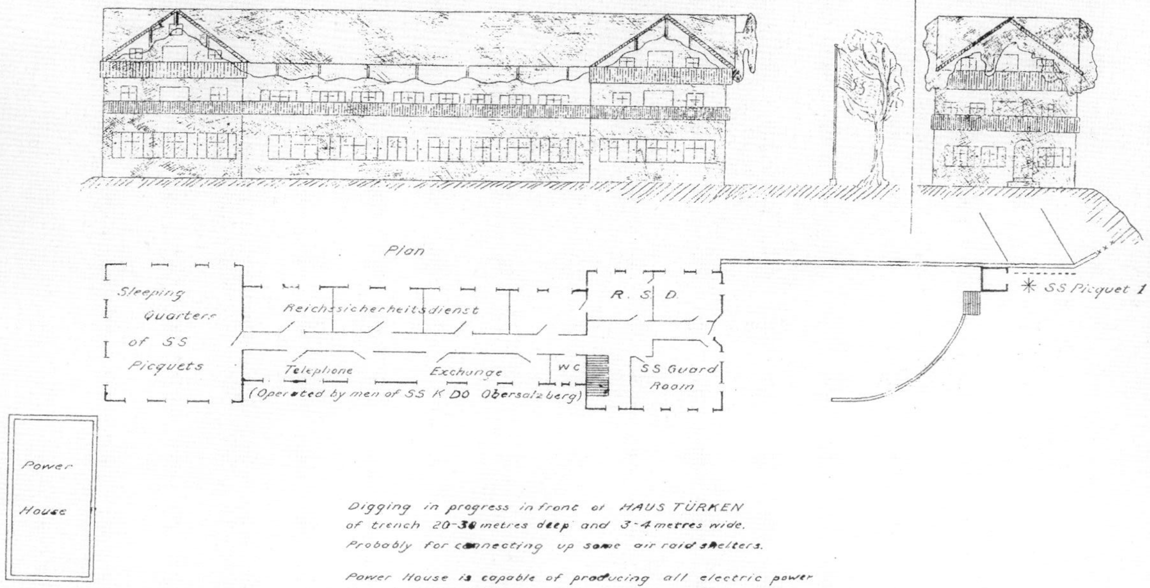

Side view
Plan
Sleeping Quarters of SS Picquets
Reichssicherheitsdienst
R. S. D.
Telephone
Exchange
(Operated by men of SS K DO Obersalzberg)
WC
SS Guard Room
SS Picquet 1
Power House

Digging in progress in front of HAUS TÜRKEN
of trench 20-30 metres deep and 3-4 metres wide.
Probably for connecting up some air raid shelters.

Power House is capable of producing all electric power
for the OBERSALZBERG in case of emergency.

Fig. 7.

ANNEX 12 : GÄSTEHAUS "HOHER GÖLL" -13-

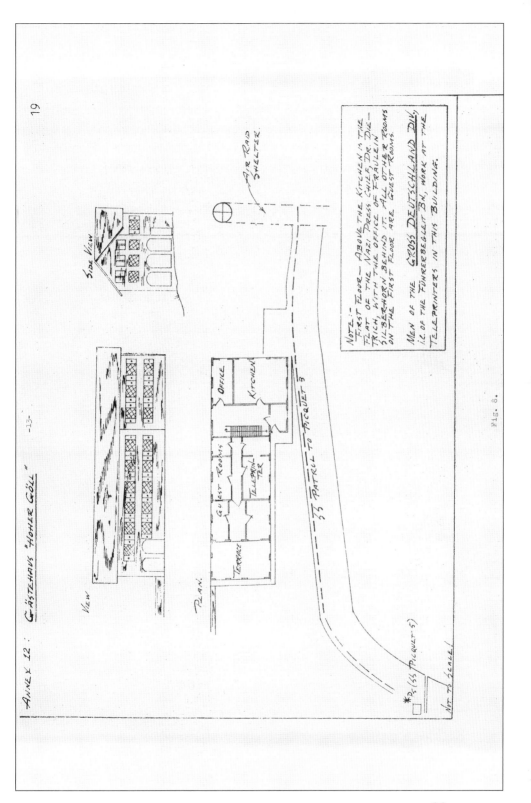

SIDE VIEW

VIEW

PLAN.

TERRACE
GUEST ROOMS
OFFICE
KITCHEN
TELEPRINTER

SS PATROL TO PICQUET 3

* P₃ (SS PICQUET 5)

NOT TO SCALE!

AIR RAID SHELTER.

NOTE:- FIRST FLOOR.- ABOVE THE KITCHEN IS THE FLAT OF THE NAZI PRESS CHIEF, DR. DIETRICH, WITH THE OFFICE OF FRAULEIN SILBERHORN BEHIND IT. ALL OTHER ROOMS ON THE FIRST FLOOR ARE GUEST ROOMS.

MEN OF THE GROSS DEUTSCHLAND DIV., i.e. OF THE FÜHRERBEGLEIT BN, WORK AT THE TELEPRINTERS IN THIS BUILDING.

Fig. 8.

55

19

Pos
Offi ce.

DAS SCHÖNE BERGHOTEL

Ein Musterbeispiel für den neuen deutschen Hotelbau: Das Gasthaus „Der Platterhof" auf dem Obersalzberg

Ein Bericht von Ernst Baumann

Das Hauszeichen des neuen Gasthauses

zeigt stilisiert das Bild der Judith Platter, der Heldin des bekannten Romans „Zwei Menschen" von Richard Voß, deren bergbauernhof früher an dieser Stelle des Obersalzbergs stand.

Bergschenke.

Inmitten der herrlichen Bergwelt des Berchtesgadener Landes:

Unweit des Berghofs, den sich der Führer erbaute, liegt unmittelbar an der deutschen Alpenstraße eines der schönsten Berghotels des Großdeutschen Reiches, das Gasthaus „Der Platterhof". Von hier aus eröffnet sich die Aussicht auf die gewaltige Runde der Berchtesgadener Felsgipfel. Weit geht der Blick vom Hohen Göll über die Pustersee-Tauern, den Watzmann mit dem Hochkalter, die Reiteralp und die mächtigen rotbraunen Wände des Untersbergs hinaus zur Feste Hohen-Salzburg und in die weite Ebene. Die Einrichtung des Hauses kann als Vorbild deutscher Wohnkultur gelten.

*

Platterhof.   Post Office.

A2019

Gästehaus, Hoher Göll.

Fig.9. Platterhof (exterior).

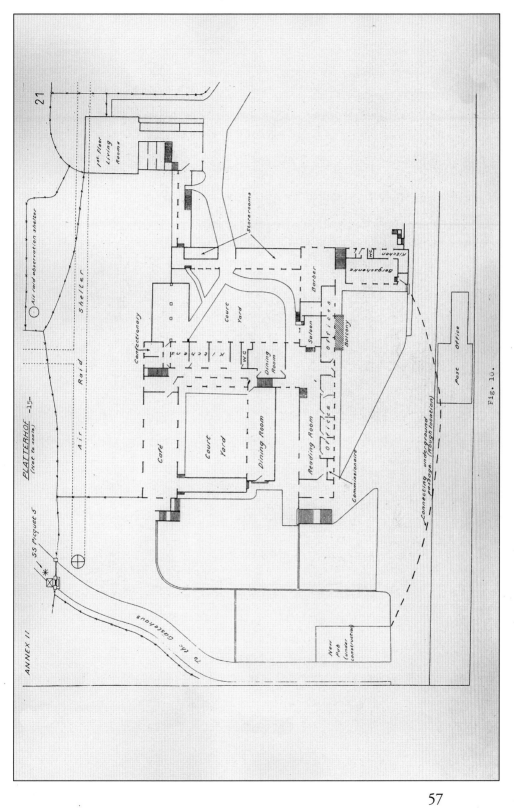

Fig. 10.

PLATTERHOF −15−
(not to scale)

21

Air raid observation shelter

1st Floor Living Rooms

Storerooms

Air Raid Shelter

Confectionary

Court Yard

Court Yard

Kitchen

Café

Dining Room

W.C.

Saloon

Border

Offices

Bergschenke

Kitchen

Balcony

Reading Room

Offices

Dining Room

Commissionaire

ANNEX 11

SS Picquet S

To the Gasthaus

New Pub (under construction)

Connecting underground passage. (Rough location)

Post Office

57

The Cafesaal (Fig.10) was, in April 1944, open to the public. There are 5 or 6 waitresses there and 3 or 4 foreign (French) waiters. Fig.11 shows the interior of the Platterhof hotel as it still was in 1944, when it was being used as a hospital.

(6) The GEFOLGSCHAFTHAUS. provides accommodation for the nurses and staff of the PLATTERHOF; the porters, clerks, etc. live at the back. There is a garage under the building for two buses (Fig.9) which take the patients in the hospital to the theatre in SALZBURG, etc.

(7) SS Barracks. The general layout of the SS barracks is shown in the sketch in Fig.12. Detailed plans, side and end elevations of the buildings, including garages and gymnasium are given in Figs.13-16. In addition to housing the SS Waehkompanie, it includes the offices of the SS-Kommando OBERSALZBERG and of the STOLLENBAUKOMPANIE (Air Raid Shelter Construction Co.).

(8) VORDERECK. (Fig.17). This consists of two houses. The first houses the Verwaltung OBERSALZ-BERG (Administrative Headquarters of the District) on the ground floor, with servants' quarters on the upper floor. Members of the Begleitkommando sleep here when HITLER is at the BERGHOF. The second house contains the LUFTSCHUTZBEFEHLSTELLE (air raid control room) which is under the direction of Untersturmführer BREDOW.

(9) MODELLBAU and KINDERGARTEN. (Fig.18). The MODELLBAU, being built into the rock, is thought to be safer than many of the other buildings and on this account is used by BORMANN as a store for his carpets. It takes its name from the model it contains of the OBERSALZBERG district.

The KINDERGARTEN takes about 20-30 children belonging to the families of officials living in the neighbourhood; BORMANN's children attend.

(10) SPAHN HAUSL. The house of Sturmbannführer SPAHN, who is in charge of the SS Administration of OBERSALZBERG, and his wife.

(11) HAUS BORMANN. The residence of the BORMANN family, consisting of BORMANN, his wife and his 9-11 children.

(12) LANDHAUS GÖRING. (Fig.19). The residence of the GÖRING family i.e. Hermann, Emma and the little Edda. The house is run by the ZICZKA family.

(13) BÜCHENHÖHE. A large settlement for children evacuated from bombed cities. It includes a fire station with quarters for fire chief Ober-scharführer WAGNER, his wife and mother.

(14) STAATLICHE BAULEITUNG. Bureau and garage of the State Office of Works.

(15) LAGER RISSENFELD. Hutments housing Czech workmen (administrative officials are German).

Eines der hundert Gastzimmer des Platterhofes.
Aus dem Fenster geht der Blick auf den Untersberg.

Im großen Speisesaal des Hauses.
Marmorsäulen tragen die holzgetäfelte Decke.

In der Empfangshalle.
Die Verwendung edler heimischer Werkstoffe und ihre sorgfältige Abstimmung aufeinander erzielen eine Wirkung, die dem Stil und der Zweckbestimmung des Hauses aufs beste entspricht. Die Einrichtung stammt von dem Münchener Innenarchitekten Professor Heinrich Michaelis.

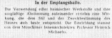

Die Frühstücksstuben sind besonders gemütlich.
Ihre Wände und Decken sind mit dem astreinen Holz der Bergzirbe getäfelt.

Am Abend in der Bibliothek.
Beim Bau des Gasthauses wurden alle Mittel neuzeitlicher Hoteltechnik benutzt. Durch die hervorragende Einrichtung und die herrliche Lage entstand hier ein vorbildliches Berg-Gasthaus.

A202

Fig.11. Platterhof (interior).

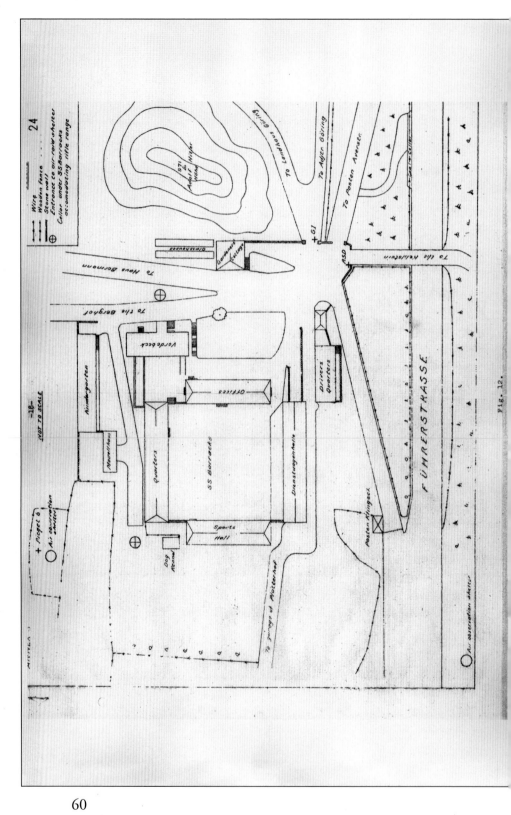

Fig. 12.

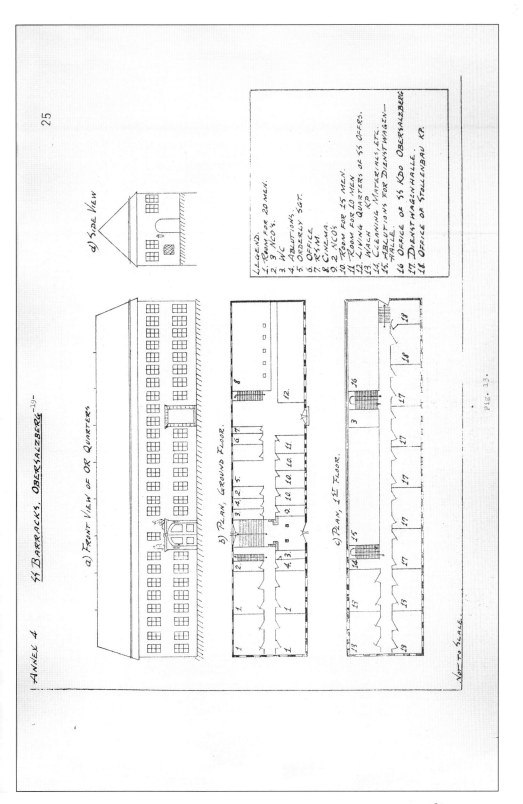

ANNEX 4

SS BARRACKS, OBERSALZBERG [19]

25

a) FRONT VIEW OF OR QUARTERS

d) SIDE VIEW

b) PLAN, GROUND FLOOR.

c) PLAN, 1ST FLOOR.

LEGEND.
1. ROOM FOR 20 MEN.
2. NCO's.
3. WC.
4. ABLUTIONS.
5. ORDERLY SGT.
6. OFFICE.
7. RSM.
8. CINEMA.
9. 2 NCO's.
10. ROOM FOR 15 MEN.
11. ROOM FOR 10 MEN.
12. LIVING QUARTERS OF SS OFFRS.
13. WACH KP.
14. CLEANING MATERIALS ETC.
15. ABLUTIONS FOR DIENSTWAGEN—HALLE.
16. OFFICE OF SS KDO OBERSALZBERG.
17. DIENSTWAGENHALLE.
18. OFFICE OF STOLLENBAU KP.

NOT TO SCALE.

FIG. 13.

61

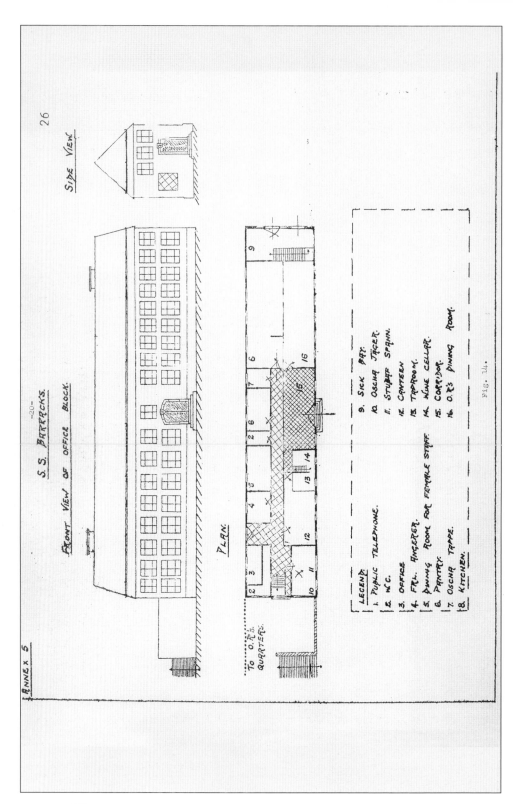

S.S. BARRACKS.
-20-

FRONT VIEW OF OFFICE BLOCK.

SIDE VIEW

26

To O.R.S. QUARTERS.

PLAN.

LEGEND:
1. PUBLIC TELEPHONE.
2. W.C.
3. OFFICE.
4. FRL. FINGERER.
5. DINING ROOM FOR FEMALE STAFF.
6. PANTRY.
7. OSCHA TRAPPE.
8. KITCHEN.
9. SICK BAY.
10. OSCHA JÄGER.
11. STURBF SPAHN.
12. CANTEEN.
13. TAPROOM.
14. WINE CELLAR.
15. CORRIDOR.
16. O.R's DINING ROOM.

Fig. 14.

S.S. BARRACKS.

FRONT VIEW OF THE DIENSTWAGENHALLE.

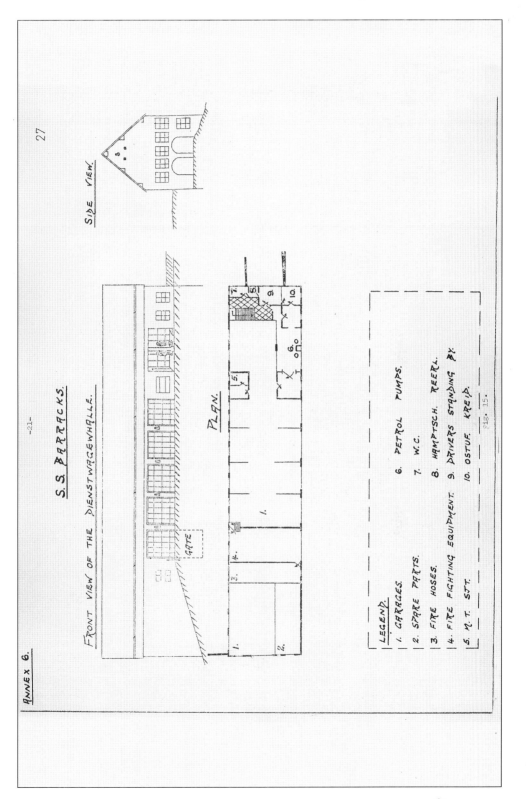

SIDE VIEW.

PLAN.

GATE

LEGEND.

1. GARAGES.
2. SPARE PARTS.
3. FIRE HOSES.
4. FIRE FIGHTING EQUIPMENT.
5. M.T. SJT.
6. PETROL PUMPS.
7. W.C.
8. HAMPTSCH. REERL.
9. DRIVERS STANDING BY.
10. OSTUF. KREIP.

Fig. 15.

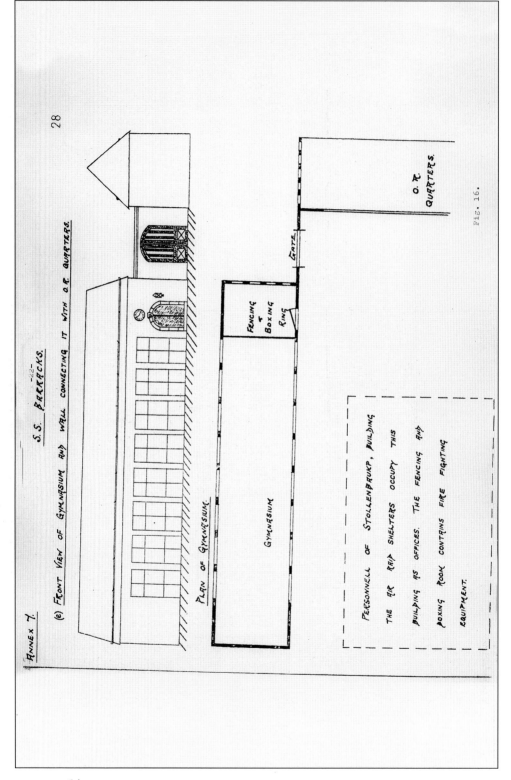

ANNEX 7.

S.S. BARRACKS.

(e) FRONT VIEW OF GYMNASIUM AND WALL CONNECTING IT WITH O.R. QUARTERS.

PLAN OF GYMNASIUM.

GYMNASIUM

FENCING + BOXING RING

GATE

O.R. QUARTERS.

PERSONNELL OF STOLLENBRUKP, BUILDING THE AIR RAID SHELTERS OCCUPY THIS BUILDING AS OFFICES. THE FENCING AND BOXING ROOM CONTAINS FIRE FIGHTING EQUIPMENT.

Fig. 16.

28

64

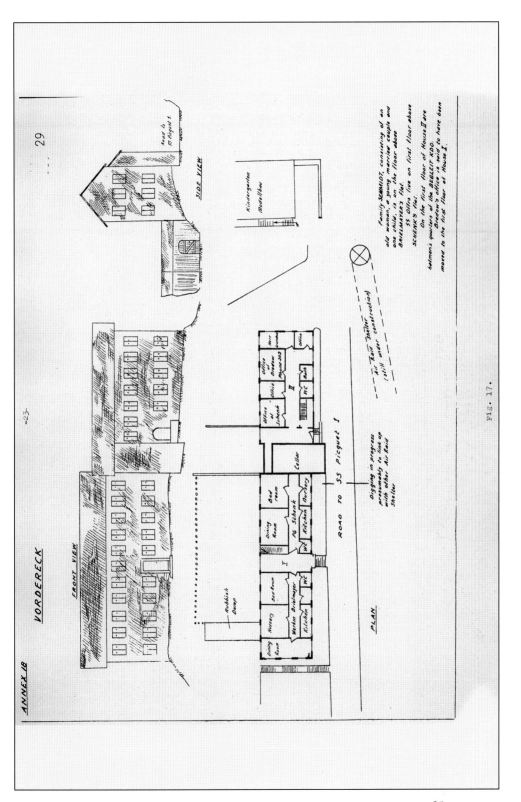

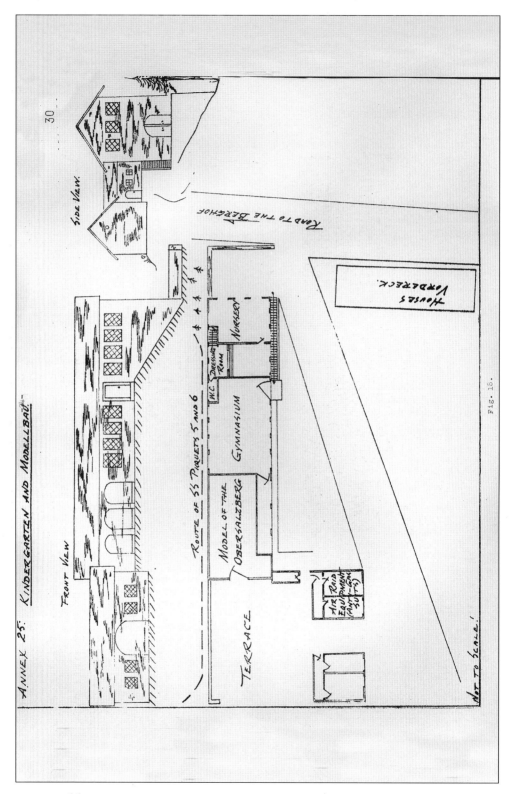

ANNEX 25: KINDERGARTEN AND MODELLBAU.

FRONT VIEW.

SIDE VIEW.

30

ROUTE OF SS PIQUETS 5 AND 6

MODEL OF THE OBERSALZBERG.

TERRACE.

GYMNASIUM.

W.C. DRESSING ROOM. NURSERY.

AIR RAID EQUIPMENT (ANT - AIR - GAS.)

ROAD TO THE BERGHOF.

HOUSES VORDERECK.

NOT TO SCALE!

Fig. 18.

ANNEX 13   LANDHAUS GÖRING

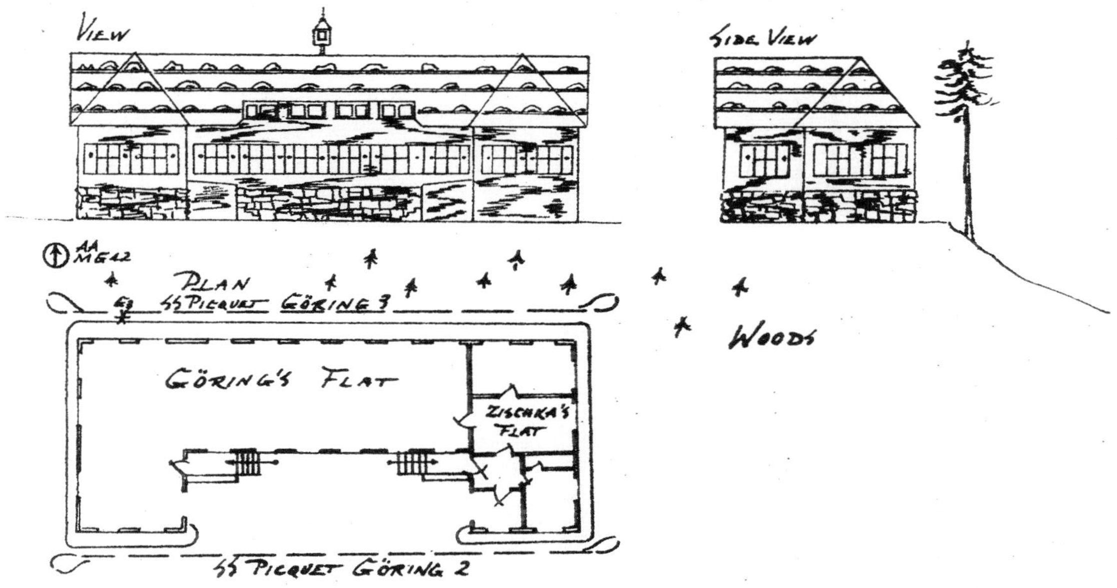

-25-

SIDE VIEW

WOODS

VIEW

$\bigoplus$ AA MG12

PLAN SS PICQUET GÖRING 3

GÖRING'S FLAT

ZISCHKA'S FLAT

SS PICQUET GÖRING 2

NOT TO SCALE

Fig. 19.

(16) KL USHOHE. This Arbeitersiedlung (workers'
settlement) consists of three rows of houses
inhabited by German workmen.

1st. row(1-6) : House 1 - Grocery shop
                            (kept by ZÖLLNER)
                 Houses 2-5 - Civilians
                 House 6 - Women working in
                            the SS barracks.

2nd. row(7-14): German workmen

3rd. row(15-22):House 18 - doctor (an SS
                            Hauptsturmführer)
                 House 22 - Herr GRÜNDER i/c
                            rations at SS barracks.

(17) HINTERECK (Figs.20a and 20b). This consists
of 3-4 houses for the accommodation of officials,
including Untersturmführer BREDOW.

(18) ADJUTANTUR GÖRING (Fig.21). This building
accommodates Göring's staff (when Göring is at the
OBERSALZBERG) and General der Flieger BODENSCHATZ,
G.F liaison officer at FHQ. It also contains one
of the three telephone exchanges on the OBERSALZBERG.

(19) GÄRTNEREI includes glasshouses for
providing vegetables and fruit for the SS in the
barracks, and gardener's cottage (see Fig.38).

(20) POST (Fig.22). The Post Office is run by
a party member (who wears the gold Party badge) with
three girl assistants, one clerk and a postman who
lost an arm in the last war.

Above the Post Office is a shop which sells
souvenirs (probably connected with the Platterhof
which is opposite - see Fig.11).

(21) KAMPFHÄUSL (Fig.23). It was here that
HITLER completed "Mein Kampf". Empty in April/May
1944. The footpath to the Platterhof is public.

(22) JUGENDVERPFLEGUNGSHEIM (Fig. 24) and the
MATERIALUS. The former was empty in April 1944; the
latter accommodated the FORZ family of which the
daughter is employed at the Post Office.

(23) THEATERHALLE OBERSALZBERG (Fig.25). A
wooden structure with gabled roof which collapsed
under the weight of snow in the winter of 1943/44.
Its reconstruction was scheduled for August 1944.
It seats 2000. The flat back of the stage is
occupied by Party member FILLHUBER.

Shows are given at 2000 hours on Tuesdays,
Thursdays and Saturdays; there is a matinee on
Saturdays at 1500 hours. Meetings are also held
there. Attendance is compulsory for the SS Wachkompanie.

(24) LAGER ANTENBERG. This camp houses the
employees of the Bauleitung OBERSALZBERG Arge and
the bauleitung HOLZMANN & FRAKE. The employees
are mostly Czechs chiefly employed on road repairs
and improvements, and, in winter, clearing the roads

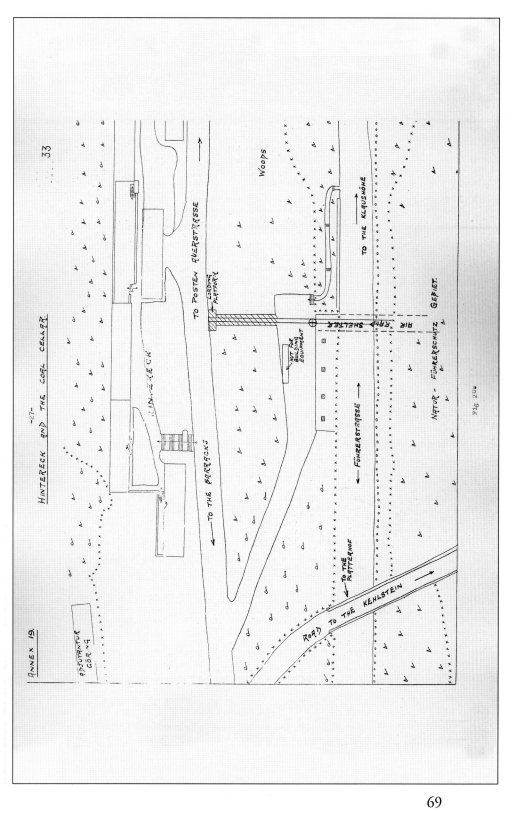

ANNEX 19.

HINTERECK AND THE COAL CELLAR.
—27—

ADJUTANTUR GÖRING

HINTERECK

TO THE BARRACKS

TO POSTEN QUERSTRASSE

LOADING PLATFORM

HUT FOR BUILDING EQUIPMENT

FÜHRERSTRASSE

AIR RAID SHELTER

TO THE KLAUSHÖHE

WOODS

NATUR-FÜHRERSCHUTZ GEBIET.

TO THE PLATTERHOF

ROAD TO THE KEHLSTEIN

Fig 2ºª

33

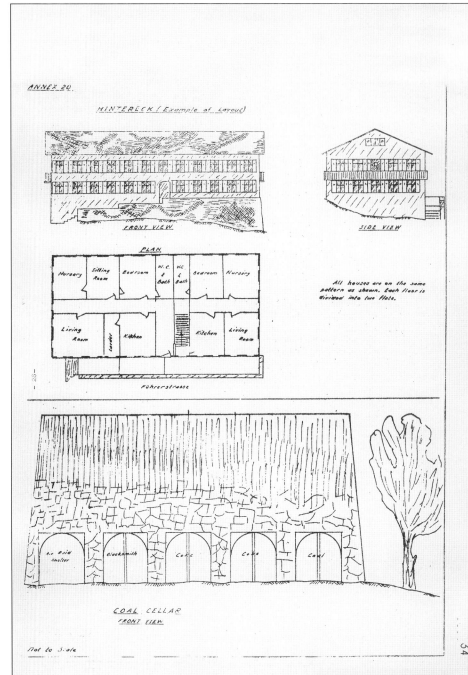

ANNEX 20.

HINTERECK (Example of Layout)

FRONT VIEW

SIDE VIEW

PLAN

| Nursery | Sitting Room | Bedroom | W.C. & Bath | W.C. & Bath | Bedroom | Nursery |

| Living Room | Larder | Kitchen | | Kitchen | Living Room |

Führerstrasse

All houses are on the same pattern as shown. Each floor is divided into two flats.

COAL CELLAR
FRONT VIEW

Air Raid Shelter | Blacksmith | Coke | Coke | Coal

Not to Scale

70

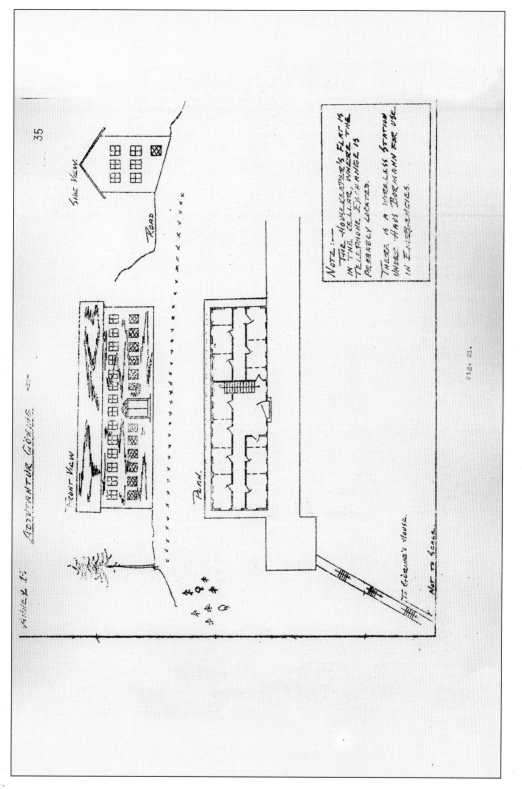

ADVENTUR GÖRING

ANNEX E.15

FRONT VIEW

SIDE VIEW

ROAD

PLAN.

TO GÖRING'S HOUSE.

NOT TO SCALE.

NOTE:—
THE HOUSEKEEPER'S FLAT IS
IN THE CELLAR, WHERE THE
TELEPHONE EXCHANGE IS
PROBABLY LOCATED.

THERE IS A WIRELESS STATION
UNDER HAUS BORMANN FOR USE
IN EMERGENCIES.

Fig. 21.

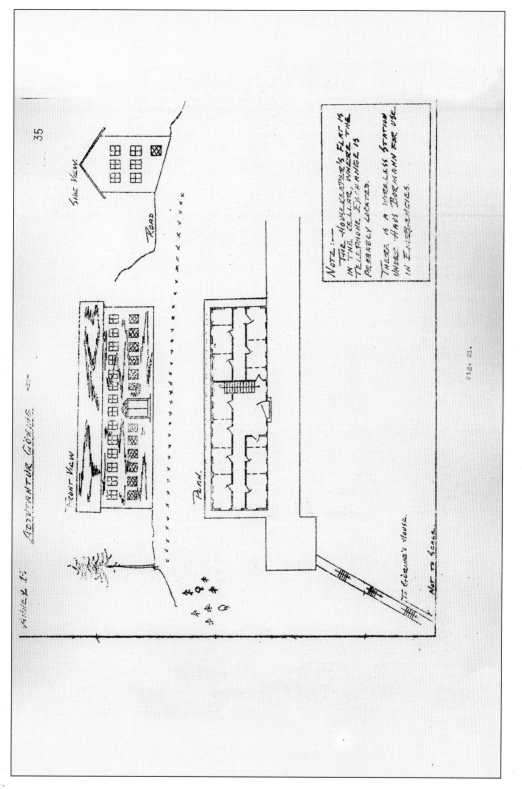

POST OFFICE OBERSALZBERG

-30-

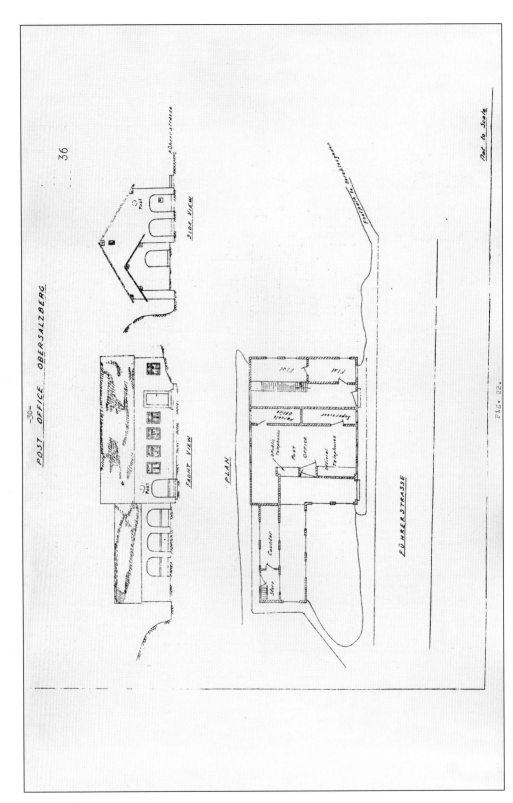

SIDE VIEW

FRONT VIEW

PLAN

FÜHRERSTRASSE

Fig. 22.

Not to Scale

72

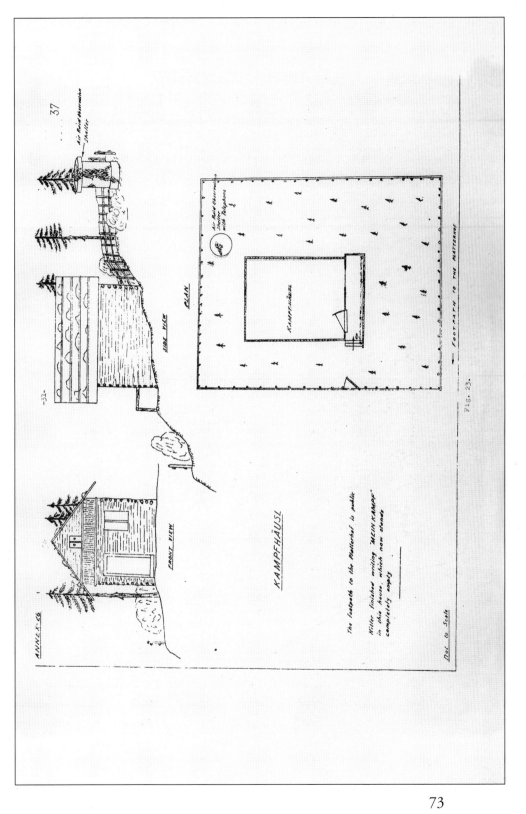

37

Air Raid Observation Shelter

-31-

SIDE VIEW

FRONT VIEW

ANNEX-66

PLAN

Air Raid Observation Shelter with Telephone

KAMPFHÄUSL

FOOTPATH TO THE PLATZERHF.

Fig. 23.

KAMPFHÄUSL

The footpath to the Platterhof is public.

Hitler finished writing "MEIN KAMPF" in this house, which now stands completely empty.

Not to Scale

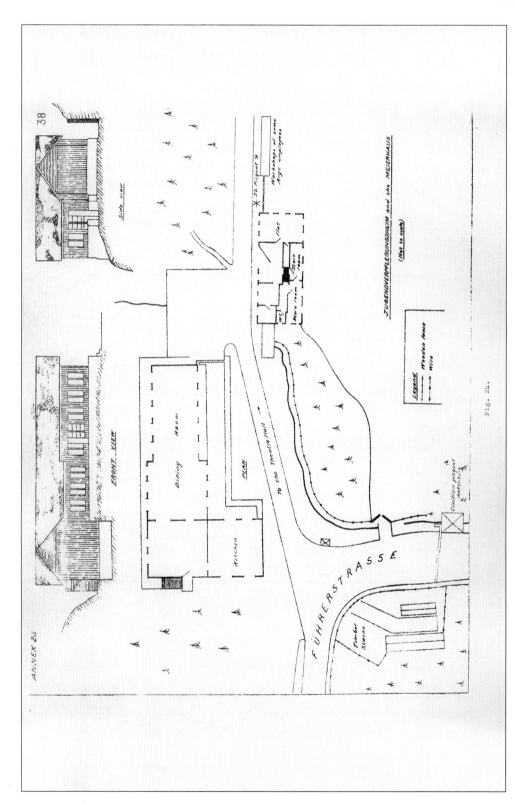

Fig. 24.

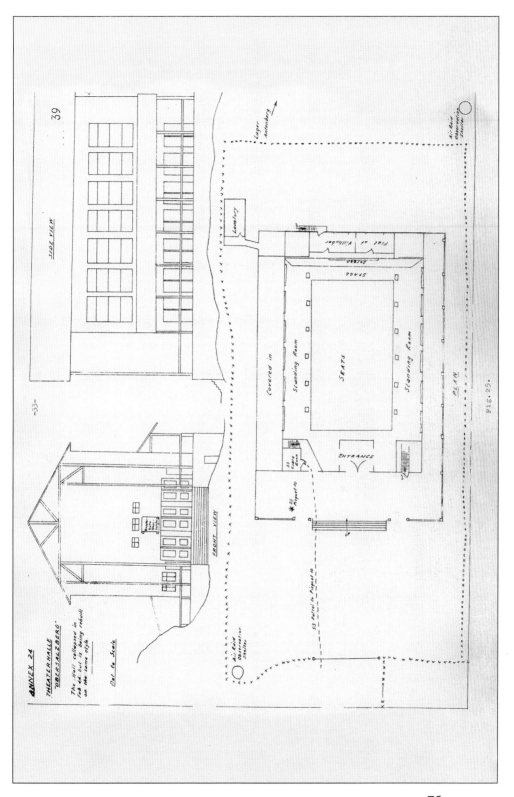

ANNEX 24

THEATERHALLE "OBERSALZBERG"

The Hall collapsed in Feb 44 but is being rebuilt on the same style

Not to Scale

SIDE VIEW

39

-33-

FRONT VIEW

Air Raid Observation Shelter

SS Patrol to Piquet 10

UP

* SS Piquet 10

SS Guard Room

ENTRANCE

Covered in

Standing Room

SEATS

Standing Room

STAGE

Flat of Villhuber

Lavatory

Lager Antenberg

Air Raid Observation Shelter

P L A N

Fig. 25.

75

of snow. Behind the camp is a dump of timber for constructional purposes and a wooden shed.

(25) BERGHAUSL, HAUS SPEER, MEISTERLEHEN and BERGHANG (Fig.26). The BERGHAUSL and the BERGHANG house civilians. HAUS SPEER is the residence of the SPEER family (wife, children and nurse of Reichminister SPEER). The MEISTERLEHEN is a dilapidated house and is unoccupied.

(26) ATELIER SPEER (Fig.27) is now used to accommodate children from bomb-damaged areas. It takes about 40 children.

(27) BAUMGARTLEHEN (Fig.28). This is the chief pigsty (Schweinstelle) of the GUTSHOF. It includes living quarters for the swineherds.

(28) GUTSHOF OBERSALZBERG (Fig.29). This, the home farm of the BERGHOF, supplies the latter with milk and butter, etc.

(29) BECKSTEIN HAUS (formerly the HESS HAUS) is now a guest house for HITLER's more important guests, e.g. the late King Boris. MUSSOLINI usually stops there when he visits the BERGHOF. It is kept by an SS Oberscharführer and his wife.

(30) TEEHAUS (MOOSLANER KOPF) is in use—unlike the Teehaus on the KEHLSTEIN which was empty in April/May 1944. It is used by HITLER as the objective of his morning walks, now that he appears no longer to visit the KEHLSTEIN.

(31) BIENENHAUS. This is the apiary belonging to the GUTSHOF.

4. Viewpoints.

The entire Führergebiet can be seen from the KEHLSTEIN, the HOHER GÖLL, the HOHES BRETT and the WATZMANN.

The BERGHOF is visible from the SCHELLENBERG-UNTERAU road and from the Cafe Rottenhöfer in BERCHTESGADEN. The DOKTORBERG near BERCHTESGADEN also commands a good view of most of the area.

A panorama of the area, taken from near BERCHTESGADEN, is shown in Fig.30.

The teahouse on the MOOSLANER KOPF is visible from the BERCHTESGADEN-UNTERAU road. The Landhaus GÖRING can be seen from OBERAU.

5. Approaches.

(1) Leave BAD REICHENHALL via the PREDIGTUHL Bahn (Fig.31) at the top of which is a hospital, formerly an hotel (Fig.32). Along the ridge of the LATTENGEBIRGE to HINTER SCHÖNAU. From SCHÖNAU to the KÖNIGSEE by train (Fig.33), up the WASSERFALL weg, avoiding Lager DÜRRECK, which is inhabited by employees of the Stollenbaukp (chiefly Roumanians). Up the HOHES BRETT. This mountain is very dangerous in winter, but can be negotiated in summer without ropes. Up to the wire south of the KEHLSTEIN BERG.

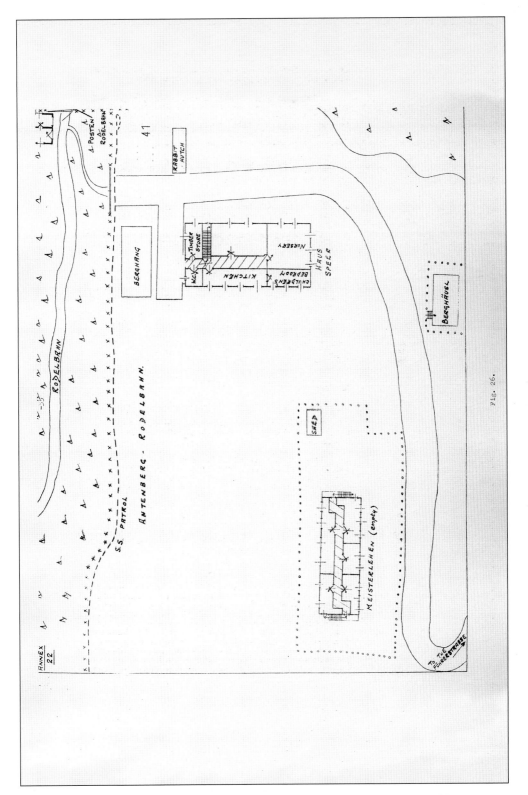

Fig. 26.

77

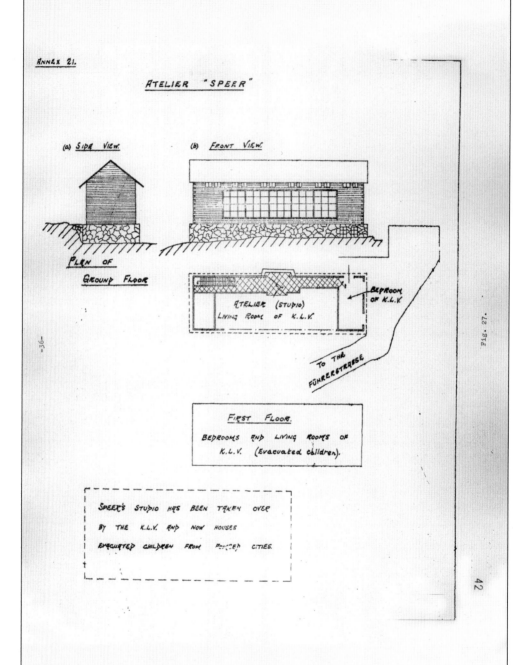

ANNEX 21.

ATELIER "SPEER"

(a) SIDE VIEW.

(b) FRONT VIEW.

PLAN OF
GROUND FLOOR

ATELIER (STUDIO)
LIVING ROOM OF K.L.V.

BEDROOM
OF K.L.V.

TO THE
FÜHRERSTRASSE

FIRST FLOOR.

BEDROOMS AND LIVING ROOMS OF
K.L.V. (Evacuated children).

SPEER'S STUDIO HAS BEEN TAKEN OVER
BY THE K.L.V. AND NOW HOUSES
EVACUATED CHILDREN FROM BOMBED CITIES.

-36-

Fig. 27.

42

78

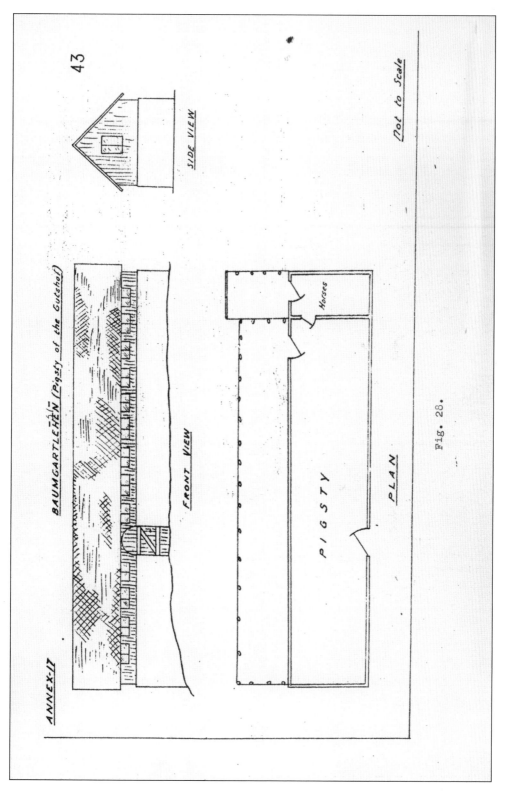

ANNEX-17

BAUMGARTLEHEN (Pigsty of the Gutshof)

SIDE VIEW

FRONT VIEW

PIGSTY

Horses

PLAN

Fig. 28.

Not to Scale

43

79

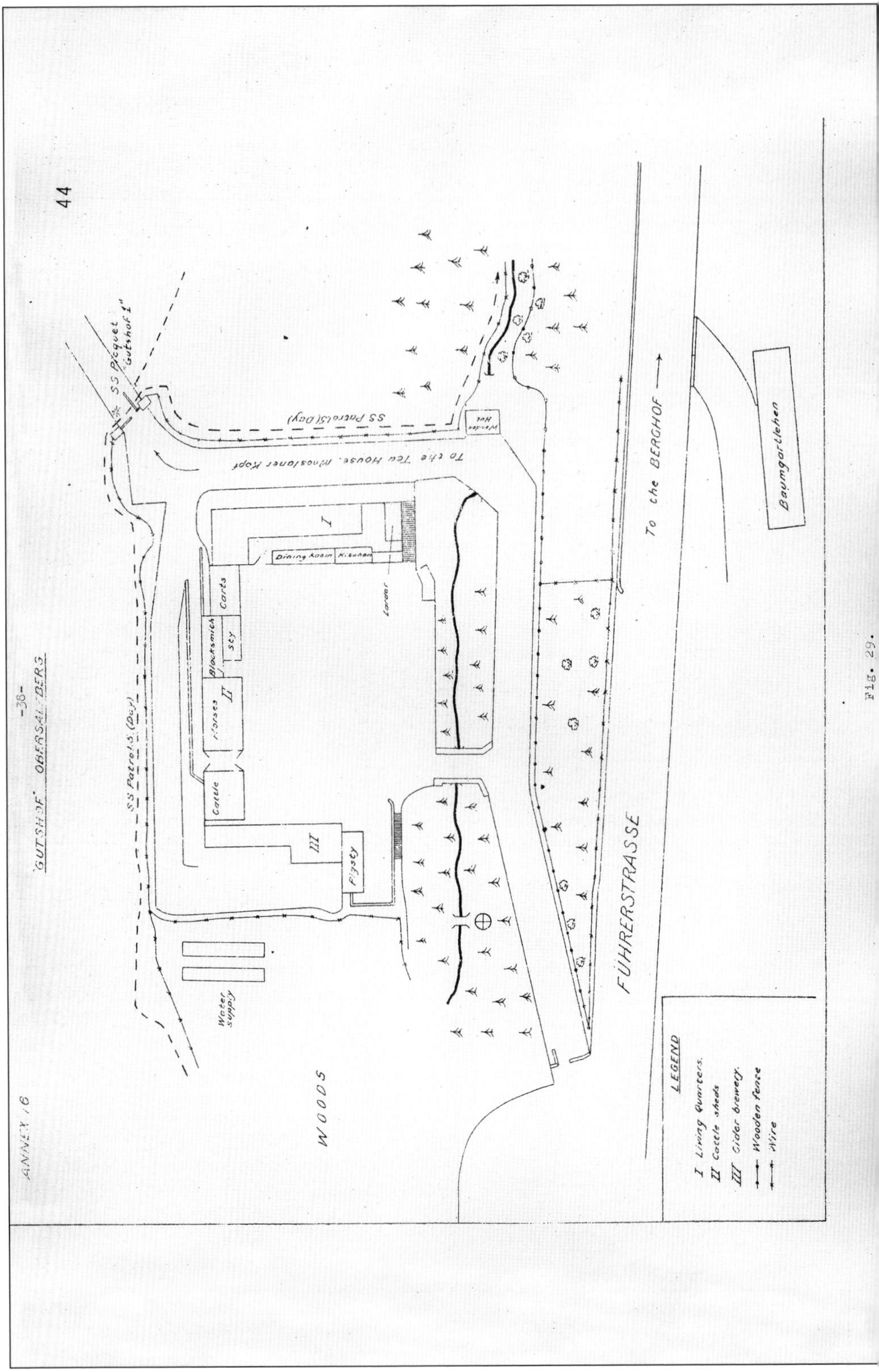
44
ANNEX 16
-38-
GUTSHOF OBERSALZBERG
SS Picquet "Gutshof 1"
SS Patrols (Day)
SS Patrols (Day)
To the Tea House, Mooslaner Kopf
Wooden Hut
I
Dining Room
Kitchen
Larder
Carts
Blacksmith
Sty
Horses
II
Cattle
III
Pigsty
Water supply
WOODS
FÜHRERSTRASSE
To the BERGHOF
Baumgartlehen
LEGEND
I Living Quarters.
II Cattle sheds
III Cider brewery.
Wooden fence
Wire

Fig. 29.

Key to Fig. 30.

1. Bergwerk.

4. Halt Berchtesgaden Ost.

11. Bahnhof (railway station).

19. Franziskaner Kirche.

23. Rathaus.

25. **Pfarrkirche.**

26. Stiftskirche.

33. Berchtesgadener Hof (Grand Hotel).

34. Protestanishe Kirche.

46. Villa Alpenglühen.

BAVARIA.

Jenner 1874

Steinernes

Café GRASSL.

Café ROTEL C

Hohes Brett

Obersalzberg

SCHIESSSTANDBRUGGE.

82

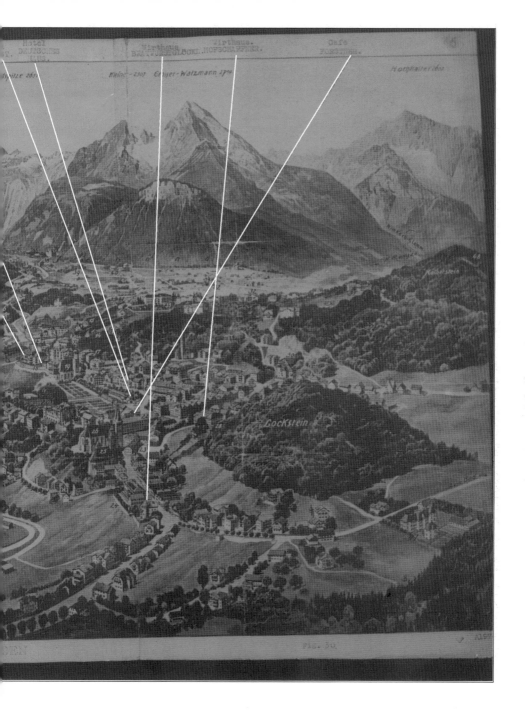

Fig. 30.

83

Fig. 31.   BAD REICHENHALL and aerial railway up to the
PREDIGSTUHL.

Fig. 32.   BAD REICHENHALL and the PREDIGSTUHL.

Fig.33. Panorama showing Berchtesgaden, Berghof, ("Hitler's Landhaus"), Schönau, Königsee and WATZMANN.

At midday and in the evening the RSD men eat, when they retire into the house and the wire can be climbed. In the evening the game-keeper has also left. Alternatively one can go via the PURSCHELLA haus on to the road leading down from the OFENER Alp or on to ROSSFELD (Fig.1). There are AA positions at both these places and there was formerly a camp for Czech workers on the OFENER ALP. This, however, no longer appears to be in existence, having collapsed under the weight of snow last winter. There are numerous small huts along the side of the road leading down from the OFENER ALP, each inhabited by two men who work the AA smoke screen, but one can get down through the woods, coming out by Lager RIEMENFELD (Fig.2).

(2) An alternative approach is to take the railway from SALZBURG to St. LEONHARD (Fig.1). Take the BERCHTESGADEN bus to UNTERAU and walk in by way of OBERAU (Fig.2).

From the Bergwerk near BERCHTESGADEN the Gutshof can be approached by way of the WASSERSCHLOSSL, (Fig.1) but dog patrols have to be reckoned with. To get into the Führergebiet (within the wire) is more difficult. The SS guard mounts at 1300 hrs, so that all reliefs take place at every uneven hour. Patrol 5 therefore arrives at the Gutshof between 1000 and 1030 hrs. On one occasion a mad woman attempted to penetrate the area. By-passing Posten TEUGELBRUNN, she climbed over the fence and got into the Gutshof, where she was arrested.

An alternative approach is by the road leading round the north of GÖRING's house (Fig.2). Getting into GÖRING's house itself is easy, as the woods are so thick that the wire can be climbed unobserved. To cross the BERGHOF road without detection, is however, out of the question.

(3) There is a path from the Bergwerk near
BERCHTESGADEN leading through two tunnels 1.80 m.
high, which cannot be missed. It follows the south
bank of the LAROSBACH (Fig.2), subsequently joining
the Auerstrasse. It is possible to cut through the
woods, travelling uphill, in the direction of the
Teehaus on the MOOSLANER KOPF. The woods north-west
of the FÜHRERGEBIET near the MOOSLANER KOPF are not,
it is reported, patrolled either by RSD or SS personnel.

Alternatively, one can go over the LAROSBACH
to the east of OBERSALZBERG (Fig.2).

Note: Fire brigade, civilian (strength about 120
      men) in UNTERAU.

* * * * * * * * * *

Use of the buses from BERCHTESGADEN itself to
the OBERSALZBERG is rather risky, as passes may be
inspected, except on the workmen's buses on which
the control is slack, the conductor merely shouting
"Every-one got passes?" and apparently being satis-
fied with a chorus of "Jawohl's", he lets every-one
get in.

The morning bus to the OBERSALZBERG leaves
BERCHTESGADEN at about 1710-1720 hrs. and the midday
bus at 1200-(1300?) hrs. There is also a workmen's
bus (red) run by the Bauleitung Arge which leaves
at 1500 hrs. The evening bus leaves at 1830 hrs,
stopping at the Bergwerk in BERCHTESGADEN (Fig.30),
UNTERAU, OBERAU (see Fig.1), KLAUSHOHE and finally
at the PLATTERHOF.

Buses leave the OBERSALZBERG at about 1000 hrs.
and 1930 hrs. The red Bauleitung Arge workmen's
bus leaves the Theaterhalle in the morning with
workers for BERCHTESGADEN whom it brings back in the
evening. (It returns at midday with the post,
except in the case of important mail which arrives
in the red mail truck (driven by an elderly man
with a gold Party badge) and is driven direct to
the Berghof).

6. Hideouts in the BERCHTESGADEN Area.

It is possible to stay at the TRIMBACHER and
GOLDENER BÄR inns in Berchtesgaden, though the
TRIMBACHER is frequented by the SS Wachkompanie,
in particular the fire-fighting platoon. Other
public houses in Berchtesgaden frequented (specially
in the evenings) by the SS Wachkompanie OBERSALZBERG
include the BRATWURSTGLÖCKL (innkeeper known as
Michel) and the HOFSCHAFFER. Wachkompanie personnel
when off duty also visit the Cafe ROTTENHOFER, the
Cafe GRASSL and the Cafe FORSTNER in Berchtesgaden.
The BRATWURSTGLÖCKL is an ordinary public house
where one can order a meal and put up for the night,
though they do not normally take people in.

The TRIMBACHER, it may be noted, is the meeting
place for most of the Czechs from Lager ANTENBERG
and Lager RIEMENFELD. (Many of these Czechs work
in Berchtesgaden as tradesmen; the barman at the
GOLDENER BÄR is a Czech from Lager ANTENBERG.

It is possible to stay, without arousing suspicion, in the Haus BRANDTNER, which is the first house on the right from the Schiessstand bridge (Figs.1 and 30) on the Berchtesgaden-Obersalzberg road, before the Villa Alpenglühen is reached. There is, however, a Gendarmerie-posten at the Schiessstandbrücke.

There are further a number of sheds on the Hoch Lenzer (Fig.1) which can be approached either from Berchtesgaden or from the Königsee via DÜRRECK (avoiding the camp at Dürreck), and in which it is possible to hide. Similarly numerous empty sheds are to be found on the way from OBERAU to the OBERSALZBERG.

Hotels at present open in Berchtesgaden include the following:

> Das Deutsche Haus,
> Zur Post, and
> Berchtesgadener Hof.

The panorama in Fig.30 shows the location of several of the above.

In regard to the Obersalzberg itself, i.e. the immediate vicinity of the Berghof, there are, or were in May 1944, a number of abandoned habitations there. These include the Kamphäusl (Fig.23) and close to it, the Jugendverpflegungsheim (Fig.24) as well as the Meisterlehen (Fig.26), though access to all three is made difficult by the wire fence surrounding the Führergebiet, whilst the Jugend-verpflegungsheim is uncomfortably close to the Führerstrasse. Both the Meisterlehen and the Jugendverpflegungsheim lie moreover in the open, unlike the Kamphäusl, which is partly surrounded by pine trees. If, as is reported, the Kamphäusl is never visited, the latter would appear to be the best hideout in the Obersalzberg itself – and a useful point from which to contact the Czech workmen in Lager Antenberg.

B. **Protection of the Obersalzberg.**

1. **Security.**

(a) **Security Personnel.** Security at the Obersalz-berg is taken care of by the Reichssicherheitsdienst (RSD). There are about 20 men under the command of Brigadeführer RATTENHUBER. He is responsible for Hitler's safety and is always at his side. He is assisted by Hauptsturmführer MÜLLER, formerly of the Waffen SS.

RSD personnel usually wear civilian clothes. At other times they wear the uniform of the Waffen SS but with the shoulder straps of the Ordnungs-polizei [+] unless they joined the RSD from the Waffen SS whose uniform they continue to wear. RSD personnel of the rank of Unterscharführer (the most common rank on the Obersalzberg) wear the Rante (a diamond-shaped patch of black cloth above the left cuff bearing the letters SD in silver embroidery.

[+] intertwined silver, brown and/or green threads.

Fig.34 shows an RSD officer of the rank of Hauptsturmführer in full dress. In winter RSD personnel
(including officers) wear the SS Gebirgsjäger
uniform shown in Fig.35b, in common with Begleitkommando and Wachkompanie personnel.

RSD men at the Obersalzberg are mostly Bavarians.

The RSD patrol the entire Führergebiet (including
the Kehlsteingebiet); they are usually accompanied
by dogs of which there are three, each under the
charge of a Hundeführer. One or two RSD men are
said to be always at the Teehaus on the Kehlstein,
which it is very difficult to reach except by the
lifts.

There is also an RSD-Kommando at Berchtesgaden,
where RSD men are always to be found hanging about
the Railway Station which is carefully watched.

(b) Passes. Passes are dark blue, and all require
a stamp (which is numbered) to be affixed every week.
Passes bear the imprint of BORMANN's or RATTENHUBER's
signature. Temporary passes may be signed by a minor
official.

Personnel of SS Wachkp OBERSALZBERG have a
special pass stating that they are members of the
coy. and allowed into the Führergebiet on duty.
They are recognised and consequently not checked.
Children under 5 require no pass. The milkman, an
employee of the Gutshof, and the woman who delivers
the secret letters are never checked.

The following system of passes was in use in
May 1944:-

(1) Führergebiet and Berghof. This pass is
inscribed "ist berechtigt, das Führergelände und
den Berghof zu betreten".

It is required in order to pass SS sentries
1 to 6 and any RSD personnel in the area.

(2) Führerstrasse. The part of the Führerstrasse
which is closed to the public runs from Posten TEUGEL-
BRUNN to Posten ANTENBERG. A special pass is required
to pass SS sentry No.8 and the TEUGELBRUNN, BERGHOF
and ANTENBERG civilian piquets. Passes of this kind
are in the possession of the Czech and German workers
employed in the area.

Passes are also possessed by the inhabitants
of the Gutshof, Beckstein Haus, Berghang, Berghäusl,
Atelier SPEER, and Haus SPEER.

The pass is marked: "ist berechtigt, die Posten
TEUGELBRUNN und ANTENBERG zu passieren".

(3) Auerstrasse. A pass is required to leave
the Führerstrasse and enter the SS barracks area
past the civilian piquet at Posten AUERSTRASSE.
This pass is marked: "ist berechtigt, Posten Auerstrasse zu passieren".

(4) Theaterhalle. A special pass is required
to attend shows at the theatre hall. Such a pass is
in the possession of every inhabitant of the OBER-
SALZBERG.

Fig.34. RSD officer of the rank of Hauptsturmführer.

Also shown in colour p. 164

(5) <u>GÖRING's House and SS Barracks area</u>. Pass
inscribed "ist berechtigt, den Posten KLINGECK zu
passieren". In the possession of all who work in
the SS barracks and the Vordereck.

Whilst GÖRING is in residence, Piquet GÖRING 1
is instructed to be particularly conscientious. All
officers who visit GÖRING must produce evidence of
having been invited. Those who wish to see GÖRING
in a hurry can go to Posten KLINGECK, where they are
taken to the RSD, and provided by the latter with a
temporary pass.

(6) <u>KEHLSTEIN</u>. To enter this area a pass must
be specially stamped "... und KEHLSTEINGEBIET".

2. <u>Troops</u>.

These include the following SS units:-
The SS Führerbegleitkommando; the SS Wachkompanie
OBERSALZBERG (SS Kommando OBERSALZBERG); the SS
Sonderkolonne (MT); and the SS Nebelabteilung
(Smoke unit).

(a). <u>SS Führerbegleitkommando</u>.
Distinction must be made between the Führerbegleitkommando (Führer's escort detachment, who are SS
personnel) and the Führerbegleitbataillon, which
usually provides the guards at FHQ/OKW, and is a
unit of the Division Grossdeutschland.*

The only Division Grossdeutschland personnel
at OBERSALZBERG are the telephone operators at the
Gästehaus Hoher G311.

The Führerbegleitkommando consists mainly of
SS officers and senior N.C.O.s with only a few other
ranks. Some are always at the Chancellery at Berlin,
others at the Berghof, and a few at FHQ, i.e. on
the Führerzug (Hitler's train). The 20 at the
Berghof live in the Vordereck and in the servants'
quarters at the Berghof.

They are distinguishable from other SS personnel
by the superior quality of their uniforms. NCOs
wear uniforms of officer pattern. Führerbegleitkommando personnel wear an arm-band above the left
cuff bearing the inscription "Adolf Hitler"; the
golden arm-band with the word "Führerhauptquartier"
is no longer worn.

Fig.35a shows the full dress uniform of a
Gruppenführer such as TIEFENBACHER, who commands
the SS Führerbegleitkommando, would wear. In winter
and on less formal occasions all ranks wear Gebirgsjäger trousers (stuffed into ski boots) and the
Bergmütze with the Totenkopf (death's head emblem)
in front, as shown in Fig.35b. The letters LAH
are worn on the shoulder straps.

The Führerbegleitkommando personnel at the
Berghof are mostly Bavarian.

---

* Guard duties at Schloss KLESSHEIM were on occasion performed
by a detachment of 2 NCOs and 20 men from the Wachkompanie,
OBERSALZBERG. It is possible that Schloss KLESSHEIM is
therefore only at times used as Führerhauptquartier.

-47-

Fig.35a.   Uniform of SS Gruppenführer TIEFENBACHER
of the SS Führerbegleitkommando.

Fig.35b.   Uniform of an Unterscharführer of the SS
Führerbegleitkommando.

Also shown in colour p. 165   91

The SS Führerbegleitkommando is commanded by
Gruppenführer TIEFENBACHER, who is also responsible
for guarding the Führer's train.

(b). SS Wachkompanie OBERSALZBERG (formerly SS Kommando
OBERSALZBERG).
The SS Kommando OBERSALZBERG or Führerschutzkommando
as it was once called, was formed in 1938 and
subsequently became the SS Wachkompanie OBERSALZBERG.
It is nominally under the direct control of Himmler.
A considerable proportion of the guard company (70%)
has been at OBERSALZBERG since the beginning of the
war. A few men have been sent from time to time to
other divisions, a practice which has become more
frequent of late. There have also been exchanges
of personnel, particularly with the SS Mountain
Division. Nowadays no-one is promoted to NCO
without previous service at the front. The personnel
vary considerably, most of them being Austrian and
Bavarian, though the nominal role also includes
Germans from the Sudetenland and Upper Silesia as
well as Volksdeutsche from Roumania.

The men are drawn from all the old SS formations
whose particular arm-bands they continue to wear on
the left sleeve. Letters denoting unit, e.g. SKD
or LAH are no longer worn on the shoulder straps.
The uniform worn by personnel of the Wachkompanie
is shown in Figs. 36 and 37.

The company was commanded (April/May 1944) by
Obersturmführer UBART, though for administrative
purposes it comes under Sturmbannführer FRANK,
commanding the SS Kommando, OBERSALZBERG. (The
duties of the SS Kommando OBERSALZBERG are purely
administrative; its strength is about 30 men, all
of whom are clerks).

The strength of the Wachkompanie is about 180
men. (For armament, see under 6. Air Raid Precautions
below).

One of the platoons is a fire fighting platoon
(Feuerlöschzug) of 3 sections, viz. one on duty,
one standing by on the Büchenhöhe and the other off
duty or performing guard duties. It is the duty of
the fire fighting platoon nightly to provide a
patrol of 3 men to check the black-out. This duty
is carried out at varying times but not after 0200 hrs.

Dress: field service, steel helmet, but no arms.

The Wachkompanie also furnishes the personnel
for the Bergwacht, a patrol of 5 to 6 men which
goes out when there is an accident in the mountains.

Reveille for the Wachkompanie is at 0700 hrs.
Field post No.; Wachkp. OBERSALZBERG 03951.

(c) SS Sonderkolonne (Dienstwagenhalle).
This is the SS unit which supplies drivers and
mechanics etc. and MT for Hitler and his entourage.
It consists of 3 Züge (platoons), viz. one Zug at
FHQ, another at PULLACH, near Munich, numbering about
40 men, and one Zug at the OBERSALZBERG, strength:
60-80 men. This platoon, in addition to providing
drivers and M.T. for Hitler's entourage also does

56

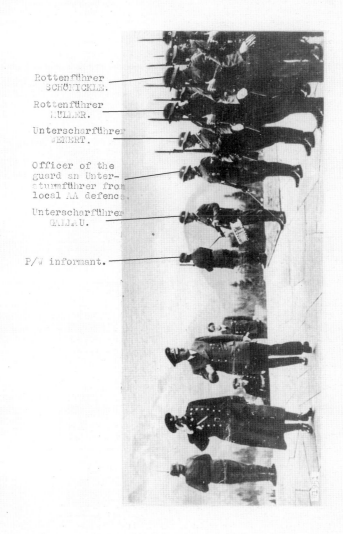

Rottenführer
SCHÖNICKLE.

Rottenführer
MULLER.

Unterscharführer
WENERT.

Officer of the
guard an Unter-
sturmführer from
local AA defence.

Unterscharführer
GAILAU.

P/W informant.

Fig.36. Guard of honour furnished by SS Wachkompanie Obersalzberg on the occasion of King Boris' last visit to the Berghof.

Fig.37.   SS Schütze of Wachkompanie in overcoat.
            (Outside Reichskanzlei, Berlin).

all the driving for the SS-Kommando OBERSALZBERG
and the Wachkompanie as well as for the Air Raid-
Shelter Construction Co., for whom they fetch
gravel from HALTHURN on the BERCHTESGADENER- BAD
REICHENHALL road. The commander of the SS Dienstwagenhalle at OBERSALZBERG is Obersturmführer
KREIDERER. Under his care are the 6 Mercedes-
Nürburg cars used by Hitler's entourage and two of
the new Hitler cars.

(d) SS Nebelabteilung.
This unit, which consists of three troops (Battalion)
each of 80-100 men, is commanded by Hauptsturmführer
SCHWEIGER, but like the Wachkompanie, comes under
the administrative control of the SS-Kommando
OBERSALZBERG. The personnel are distributed about
the countryside, two to a hut. Smoke equipment
consists of small holders, a gas flask and a stove
pipe. The apparatus is put into operation by
turning a handle, except for apparatus in the
Führergebiet, which is operated electrically.

3. Piquets and Patrols.(see Fig.2).

Two types of piquets and patrols exist at the
OBERSALZBERG, viz. SS and civilian.

(a) SS piquets and patrols.
These are provided by the SS Wachkompanie OBERSALZBERG.

(1) SS piquets (see Fig.2).

No.	Place.	Weapons.	Remarks.
1.	Haus Türken	Automatic pistol(FN)	-
2.	In front of the Berghof.	"	Only at night. A number of RSD personnel in vicinity piquet very strictly.
3.	At entrance to the Berghof.	"	Alarm devices to Haus Türken When Hitler is at the Berghof there is also an Untersturm-führer at this post. On arrival at this gate Hitler's chauffeur gives one toot on the horn, Bormann's chauffeur two and the gate is thrown open.
4.	Behind servants' quarters at Berghof.	"	-
5.	Gästehaus.	Rifle '98.	It is possible to get into the back of the Berghof through the Gästehaus.
6.	"Idiotenhügel" be-tween Gästehaus and and Berghof.	"	Has good view of approach from Berghof to Gästehaus.
7.	?		Presumably no longer exists.
8.	At loading ramp to Führerstrasse.	"	
9.	Maierhaus.	Automatic pistol(FN)	-
10.	Theaterhalle.	Rifle '98.	Six men-reliefs for sentries in the theatre hall itself. During a show RSD personnel and entire Bereitschaft (squad ready to turn out for duty at any time) of the Wachkompanie as well.

SS piquets (contd.).+

No.	Place	Weapons	Remarks.
G1.	At gate to Gärtnerei (see Fig.38)	Pistol	When GÖRING is in residence the piquet exercises stricter control.
G2.	In front of GÖRING's house.	Machine pistol	Night and day because of air raid shelter.
G3.	Behind GÖRING's house.	MG34 on tripod	Only at night.
	Gutshof.	Rifle '98	Chief duty to watch over Hitler during his early morning walks (to Teehaus) Can see Hitler for part of walk at distance of 800-1000 m. Kept informed of morning walks.

It is possible that the system of piquets described above has been revised since April/May 1944 and that sentries are instead now placed at the entrances to the air raid shelters which were under construction at that time (see Fig.2, etc.).

(2) SS patrols. These are on one-man patrols. All patrols carry rifles and are relieved every 2 hrs. Some of the routes taken by the patrols are given below:-

Patrol 1: BERGHOF to MOOSLANER KOPF. The patrol is relieved at the BERGHOF. The beat takes 15-20 minutes. Patrol chats for a long time with the civilian piquet at the MOOSLANER KOPF.

Patrol 5: SS piquet post 3 to civilian piquet at TEUGELBRUNN. Patrol crosses bridge over stream until he is within sight of the civilian piquet at TEUGELBRUNN but he does not go right up to his post. By night he patrols up to the MOOSLANER KOPF. (Alarm telephone and bells on trees).

Patrol Gästehaus to Piquet Post 3.

Patrol Posten ANTENBERG to Posten RODELBAHN. Patrol along wire. He can see down to the Führerstrasse except where it is screened by trees.

Patrol Bienenhaus: Operates only when Hitler is at the Berghof.

Patrol Kehlstein: When Hitler is at the Berghof, area north of Kehlstein patrolled in winter by one pair of SS guards at a time.

+ Extra piquets are provided when Hitler is at the Berghof viz. one in front of and outside his study and another behind the Berghof.

(b) <u>Civilian piquets and patrols.</u>   60

(1) <u>Civilian piquets.</u> These are mostly
Bavarian or Austrian. They look like ordinary
workmen and are a very mixed type, but reliable
Nazis of high standing. They stand on duty in
sentry huts (see Fig.39) and wear civilian clothes
without any distinguishing marks. Apparently they
are not armed. Civilian piquets are stationed at
the following points:-

　　　　(i)   Posten TEUGELBRUNN
　　　　(ii) Posten AUERSTRASSE
　　　　(iii) Posten RODELBAHN (wooden sentry box)
　　　　 Easy to get past piquet if approached
　　　　 in the right way.
　　　　(iv) Posten ANTENBERG. Stands in open to
　　　　 check traffic entering and leaving
　　　　 ANTENBERG.
　　　　(v)   SS Barracks. Two civilian piquets
　　　　 are on duty at the KLINGECK.

(2) <u>Civilian patrols.</u> The only civilian patrols
are the lumberjacks and a gamekeeper who wander round
the KEHLSTEIN.

4. <u>Wire.</u> (see Fig.2).

Fences in and around the FÜHRERGEBIET are built
of mesh wire and are 200/220 cm. (about 7ft.) high;
they are supported by steel tubes placed at intervals
of 3-5 m. The tubes are bent over inwards at the
top, the bent part carrying 3-4 strands of barbed
wire.

There are numerous gates in the wire - also
of wire mesh - all of which are locked except those
covered by guards. There is no electric current in
the wire. As far as is known there are no trip
wire or automatic alarm apparatus.

The KEHLSTEINGEBIET is also completely wired off.

5. <u>Anti-Aircraft Protection.</u> (see Figs.1, 2, 30).

Anti-aircraft guns are sited as follows:-

(a) At the end of the road leading to the OFENER ALP
    (part of a troop)
(b) Directly next to the ROSSFELD Hütte (remainder of
    above troop).
(c) At SCHÖNAU (one troop, men of which are billeted
    at the KOHLHIASL, an inn).
(d) Directly opposite the Bergwerk at BERCHTESGADEN.
    at the far side of the Ache in bend of the
    river (one troop).
(e) At the Dietrich Eckart Hütte near DÜRRECK (one
    troop).
(f) On the LOCKSTEIN, BERCHTESGADEN.

The guns are mostly 8.8 cm. calibre. There
are no searchlights. There is also a section of
4-barrelled A.A. guns on the OBERSALZBERG. (see Fig.2).
All A.A. troops are under the administration of the
SS-Kommando OBERSALZBERG.

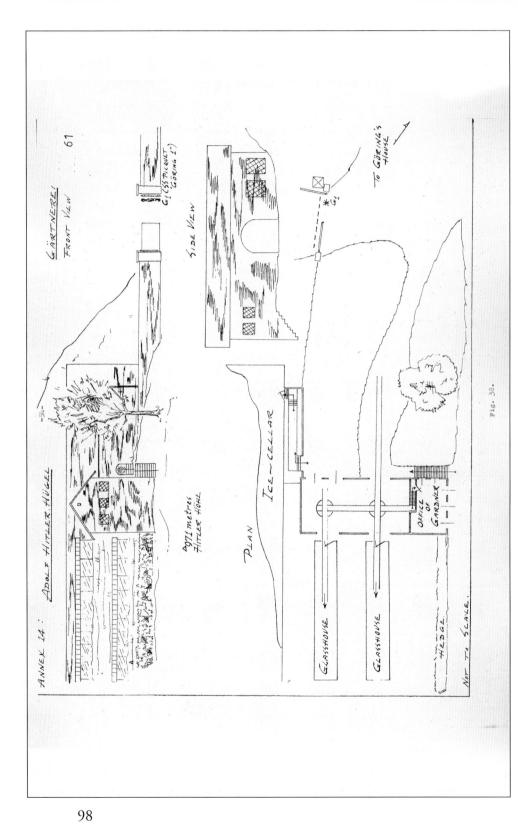

ANNEX 14: ADOLF HITLER-HÜGEL

GÄRTNEREI
FRONT VIEW

61

G₁ (SS PICQUET "GÖRING 1")

SIDE VIEW

971 metres
HITLER HÖHE

PLAN

ICE-CELLAR

GLASSHOUSE

GLASSHOUSE

HEDGE

OFFICE OF GARDNER

G₁

TO GÖRING'S HOUSE

NOT TO SCALE.

Fig. 38.

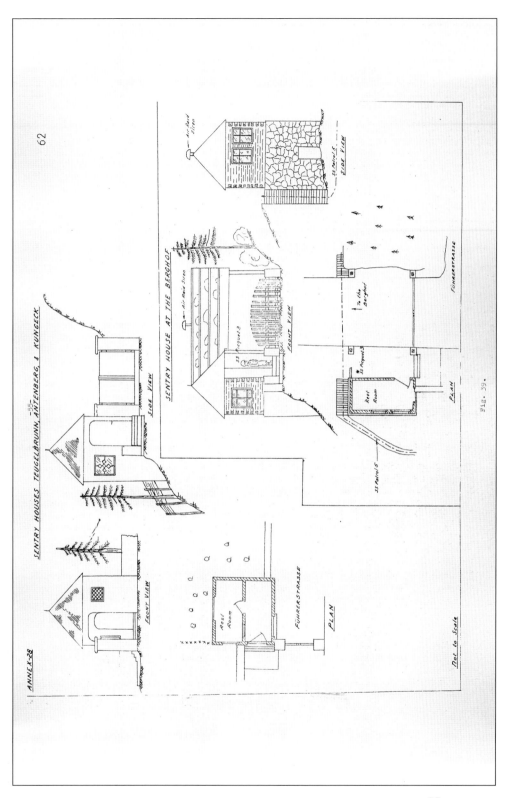

SENTRY HOUSES TEUGELBRUNN, ANTENBERG, & KUNGECK

ANNEX-28

SENTRY HOUSE AT THE BERGHOF

62

99

6. Air Raid Precautions.

(a) Warning System.

Warning of enemy aircraft is received direct from
the Warnkommando, Travenstein and from the Party
Chancellery at MUNICH. The warning system for
OBERSALZBERG is under the control of Untersturm-
führer BREDOW with HQ in the second house of the
VORDERECK.

Sirens are installed at the PLATTERHOF; at
House 20 on the KLAUSHÖHE and probably at the
BUCHENHÖHE. They give the following signals:-

(1) Vorwarnung (Alert) also called the
"Offentliche Luftwarnung" (Public Alert): 3 deep
long blasts lasting one minute in all. This means
single aircraft over the area or aircraft in direct
flight towards the area but some distance away.

(2) Flieger Alarm: Wailing sound signifying
aircraft in area (given even when a few aircraft
have become detached from formations attacking
MUNICH, for example).

(3) Vorentwarnung: (First All Clear). As
for (1) signifying that main body of raiders has
passed.

(4) Entwarnung: (Second All Clear). High-
pitched blast lasting one minute.

When the public alert is sounded a special
warning in the form of 3 short rings repeated twice
is given on the following telephones:-

Ext. 383 U.v.D. (Unteroffizier vom Dienst)
                or orderly NCO.
Ext. 369 Fencing Room i.e. fire piquet
Ext. 333 Equipment (fire-fighting) room.

The above extensions are at the SS Barracks.

Also Ext. 202 (Untersturmführer BREDOW).
      Ext. 283 Klaushöhe. Fire-fighting squad.

(b) Air Raid Shelters. (see Fig.2).

Vast air raid shelters were built into the mountain
side at OBERSALZBERG in 1943/44. HITLER's and
BORMANN's shelters were completed in May 1944. All
shelters are to be linked up.

HITLER's shelter runs under the Berghof and is
15-20 m. underground: it zig-zags at the entrance,
turning left, left again, then right, where it
reaches the main passage. The shelter itself is
80-100 m. long with rooms leading off at either side.
It has a parquet floor and carpets, and is sumptuously
furnished and centrally heated by a boiler built-in
underneath the shelter. The shelter is ventillated
but there are no air shafts. It has 3 exits.

In addition to air raid shelters there are
several observation shelters on the OBERSALZBERG
(see Fig.23). Protection consists of 15-20 cm. of
reinforced concrete. It was reported in April 1944
that they were all to be connected by telephone.

(c) <u>Camouflage</u>. Apart from being treated to
resist fire, all buildings at the OBERSALZBERG
are reported to be sprayed with paint in a
disruptive pattern which is changed every 3 months.

C. <u>Personalities in the OBERSALZBERG and their habits</u>.

1. <u>Hitler</u>.

(a) <u>Appearance</u>. Photographs of Hitler, who is now
55, often show such changes in appearance that one
is tempted to credit the popular belief that he has
one or more doubles. Thus the air of good health,
calm and collected bearing mentioned by officers
<u>visiting</u> FHQ in 1943 contrasts with the description
of officers actually serving there at the time,
that the Führer was looking 10 years older. The
photograph in Fig.40 showing the Führer in his train
was taken in 1943 and bears out the report at first
hand of Hitler looking grey and bent in May 1944;
yet the photographs in Figs.41a and 41b of Hitler
after the attentat of July 20th, 1944, indicate the
very reverse. How much these changes in appearance
are to be ascribed to the frequent injections given
the Führer, who is in general well-known to enjoy
poor health, or to the employment of a double, it
is impossible to say, evidence on the latter point
being particularly conflicting.

Hitler's dress varies from the greenish-khaki
jacket and breeches seen in Fig.36 for instance,
such as he usually wears out-of-doors on formal
occasions, to the brown or grey double-breasted
jacket and black trousers that he normally affects
indoors and at the Berghof.

Apart from the Iron Cross Hitler wears no
military decorations.

Fig.40.

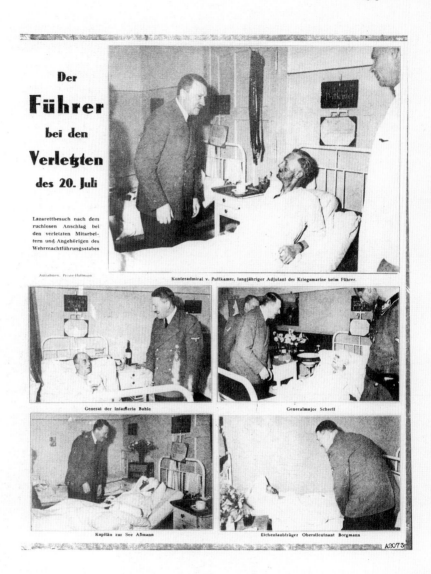

Der
Führer
bei den
Verletzten
des 20. Juli

Lazarettbesuch nach dem ruchlosen Anschlag bei den verletzten Mitarbeitern und Angehörigen des Wehrmachtführungsstabes

Aufnahmen: Presse-Hoffmann

Konteradmiral v. Puttkamer, langjähriger Adjutant der Kriegsmarine beim Führer.

General der Infanterie Buhle

Generalmajor Scherff

Kapitän zur See Aßmann

Eichenlaubträger Oberstleutnant Borgmann

A2073

Fig.41a.

Reichsleiter General Ritter von Epp machte sich zum Sprecher der Parteiführerschaft, indem er mit bewegten Worten der Freude Ausdruck gab, den Führer nach dem ruchlosen Anschlag vom 20. Juli in voller Gesundheit und Schaffenskraft zu sehen.

Von links: Reichsleiter General Ritter von Epp, Reichsführer ⚡ Himmler, der Reichsbevollmächtigte für den totalen Kriegseinsatz, Reichsminister Dr. Goebbels, Reichsleiter für die Presse Amann, Reichsminister Dr. Frick, Reichsarbeitsführer Hierl, Reichsminister Rosenberg, Reichsleiter Bouhler und Reichsleiter von Schirach.

Der Befehlshaber des Heimatheeres, Reichsführer ⚡ Reichsinnenminister Himmler, im Gespräch mit dem Reichskommissar für Norwegen, Gauleiter Terboven.

Der Chef des Wehrmachtführungsstabes, Generaloberst Jodl, unterhält sich mit Reichsminister Backe und Gauleiter Hofer.

Der Führer spricht mit dem Generalbevollmächtigten für den Arbeitseinsatz, Gauleiter Sauckel.
Aufnahmen: Presse-Hoffmann

Der Führer verabschiedet sich nach der Kundgebung der Treue und des gläubigen Vertrauens, die ihm die Parteiführerschaft bereitete.

A2071

Fig.41b.

103

(b) <u>Hitler's doubles</u>. Evidence is conflicting of the truth of this popular rumour. The only confirmation comes second-hand from a Gestapo official, who describes in some detail his surprise at seeing the Führer pass him twice (in the same direction) within a few minute s at the Reichkanzlei in Berlin and first-hand from a number of the Wach-kompanie of the SS Leibstandarte Adolf Hitler. In the latter instance, the double is described as a Ministerialgehilfe employed at the Reichskanzlei, Berlin, who wore the prescribed uniform of brown jacket and black trousers and was so much the exact double of Hitler as frequently to be mistaken for him and saluted by the SS guards. It is possible that it is this person who was referred to by the Führer as the "collaborator BERGER" killed in the bomb attempt on Hitler's life of July 20th 1944 at MÜNSINGEN (another of the FHQs). On the other hand the evidence of another SS Leibstandarte man who was one of Hitler's three body servants from 1936-1940 refutes the above report of one or more doubles.

(c) <u>Routine at the Berghof</u>. Hitler is a late riser, never getting up before 0900 or 1000 hrs. He is first seen by his barber, after which he either goes for his morning walk to the MOOSLANER KOPF, or attends a conference. He always walks alone +
to the MOOSLANER KOPF, strolling in a fairly leisurely manner. The walk takes 15 to 20 mins. at normal pace. There is an SS guard at each end and an SS patrol (one man) patrolling the route. Hitler cannot bear to feel himself watched, and if he sees an SS man following him about, he shouts at him "If you are frightened, go and guard yourself". In consequence guards have been instructed to keep him in sight but to remain unobserved themselves. This order has, however, been countermanded and reinforced several times. When Hitler is on this early morning walk an RSD official patrols the area with a dog. The route taken by Hitler on this walk to the MOOSLANER KOPF is shown in Fig.2.

When Hitler arrives at the Teehaus on the MOOSLANER KOPF, the SS guard or RSD official who is there on such occasions phones for the Kolonne,x (cars, adjutants, RSD, etc.), who meet him there. The tea-room is opened for him and he takes breakfast. Hitler <u>never</u> walks back, but drives with his Kolonne past the piquet Gutshof 1 along the Führerstrasse past piquet 3 into the Berghof.

+ In contrast with earlier days (1940) when it appears to have been Hitler's practice to take his walk at 1500 hrs. accom-panied by BORMANN and SCHAUB (his personal adjutants) as well as by his aides-de-camp, the average number of the party rarely being less than twelve. The party was followed at a discreet distance by 6-10 guards. Two SD men were on duty at the Teehaus itself, where Hitler remained till 1830 or 1900 hrs.

x This Kolonne consisted in 1940 (when the same practice was that described above obtained) of 4-6 cars; Hitler always travelled in the leading car.

Otherwise Hitler breakfasts between 1100 and 1130 hrs. Breakfast normally consists of milk and toast. (Keks).

In the afternoon Hitler receives visitors: bearers of the Knights Cross, artists and other personalities, the arrival of whom must be previously notified. Dr. MORELL sometimes sees him in the morning.

If he has official visits he leaves by road for SCHLOSS KLESSHEIM at 1200 hrs. The cars are mostly Mercedes-Nürburg 6-seaters (see Appendix.). Hitler himself has two or more cars, which are armour-plated, with wind screen and side-screens 2 ins. thick. Colour: dark blue. Flies Führer's pennant on the right mudguard.

1600 hrs. - lunch. Vegetables only. Hitler would sometimes invite GÖRING or BORMANN's family to lunch.

After lunch Hitler works until 2200 hrs. usually with Eva BRAUN, who is fetched by telephone from the Gästehaus, or with a clerk.

2200 hrs. - conference on the military situation. The generals etc. used to arrive by car, via BAD REICHENHALL and BERCHTESGADEN, entering the Berghof at piquet post 3, where they were all checked. They were stopped first by the gendarme at the SCHIESSSTANDBRÜCKE, who noted who they were, as they had no pass, and telephoned Posten TEUGELBRUNN, who in turn telephoned piquet 3. Generals were sometimes asked for a lift by personnel of the Wachkp. who found themselves at the SCHIESSSTAND-BRÜCKE.

0100 - 0130 Hitler has supper. As for lunch.
0300 - 0400 or later he goes to bed.

When arriving at or departing from OBERSALZBERG, Hitler always travels by his special train, which has a quadruple 2 cm. AA gun at each end. He usually drives down to SCHLOSS KLESSHEIM, and leaves from there; sometimes, however, from BERCHTESGADEN via BAD REICHENHALL. The train is usually stationed at SCHLOSS KLESSHEIM. There are three other special trains, - RIBBENTROP's, KEITEL's (which is stationed at BISCHOFSWIESEN, where there is supposed to be a magnificent chancellery), and the guest train which fetches guests from SALZBURG or from the aerodrome at AINRING to BERCHTESGADEN.

Hitler used to go up the KEHLSTEIN at one time but seems to have dropped this practice of late.

+ See attached Appendix. I...Hitler's Cars.

x Up to 1940, lunch was served at 1400 hrs.; dinner being served between 1930 and 2130 hrs.

2. Other personalities in the OBERSALZBERG.

(a) Martin BORMANN. (Fig.42). Born 1900. Chief of
Staff of the Chancellery of the Party (Stabsleiter
der Partei-Kanzlei) and member of the War Cabinet,
BORMANN simultaneously holds the rank of SS Gruppenführer and SA Gruppenführer. By calling a farmer,
he became, after World War I, a member of the notorious
Rossbach Freikorps and was connected with several
FEME murders. Until 1941 he was HESS's right hand
man and succeeded HESS in office after the latter's
flight to Scotland. BORMANN is in supreme control
of the OBERSALZBERG in Hitler's absence. He is not
popular and is known locally as the "Black Shadow
on the Mountain" (Schwarzer Schatten am Berg). He
rarely leaves the OBERSALZBERG and nearly always
wears civilian clothes, viz. grey trousers tucked
into boots, grey jacket and soft hat.

        Frequently seen in 3-axle touring car (usually
with a horde of children in the back), which he
drives himself. He does not drive nor permit others
to drive at over 30 m.p.h. in the OBERSALZBERG.

Fig.42.
(Bormann in centre).

(b) Heinrich HIMMLER. A rare visitor to the Berghof
which he visited for instance in the period August
1943 - May 1944 only twice, being accompanied on one
occasion by SS Oberstgruppenführer Sepp.DIETRICH.
Moved about everywhere without a guard and was not
challenged in any way by the patrols. On both
occasions he left the same day as he arrived.

(c) Hermann GÖRING. GÖRING is the successor
designate to Hitler, Chairman of the War Cabinet,
member of the Privy Council, Reich Minister for Air etc.

He is a fairly frequent visitor to the OBERSALZBERG
where he stays, at times for considerable periods,
at the Landhaus Göring. He is always accompanied
by a Luftwaffe Feldwebel (Sergeant), and his chauffeur
is an Oberleutnant of the Luftwaffe. General der
Flieger BODENSCHATZ is his frequent companion though
GÖRING walks about a good deal alone. Does not
appear to be carefully guarded.

(d) Joachim von RIBBENTROP. Reich Minister for
Foreign Affairs; member of the Privy Council.
Rarely goes nearer to the Berghof than SCHLOSS
KLESSHEIM. He has a villa at FÜSCHL.

(e) Albert SPEER. Reich Minister for Armaments
and War Production and Chief of the Organisation
Todt, etc. Is rarely at the OBERSALZBERG although
his family reside there in the Haus Speer.

(f) Dr. Otto DIETRICH holds the rank of SS Gruppenführer and is Reich Press Chief of the Nazi Party.
He is a frequent visitor to the OBERSALZBERG
where he stays at the Gästehaus HOHER GÖLL. As
Staats-Sekretär in the Reich Ministry of Propaganda,
he is GOEBBELS's representative at BERCHTESGADEN.
Frequently seen in uniform as well as in mufti.

(g) Julius SCHAUB (Fig.43) holds the rank of SS
Obergruppenführer and is one of Hitler's personal
adjutants. His place at the OBERSALZBERG appears
to be taken by Brigadeführer ALBRECHT as he is
rarely seen there nowadays.

Fig.43.

(h) Alwin ALBRECHT is like SCHAUB a persönlicher
Adjutant des Führers and holds the rank of NSKK
Brigadeführer. He generally wears uniform.

(i) RATTENHUBER holds the rank of Brigadeführer
and the post of Chief of the Reichsicherheitsdienst
at the OBERSALZBERG. Age about 50; lives in the
Gästehaus HOHER GÖLL. He is responsible for Hitler's
safety and rarely leaves his side.

(j) <u>Eva BRAUN</u>, Hitler's secretary. Age about 24; brunette, attractive and unconventional in her costume, sometimes wearing Bavarian leather shorts. Walks around with two black dogs, generally in the company of Frl. SILBERHORN, telephone operator at the Gästehaus, when off duty. Several RSD personnel always in the background when she goes out. Unapproachable, no make-up (Hitler, it appears cannot tolerate the use of cosmetics). Until 1942, (if not later) lived in the Berghof. Relations with Hitler now appear to be of a platonic nature.

(k) <u>General der Flieger Karl BODENSCHATZ</u>, is the Chief of GÖRING's personal staff and resides in the Adjutantür Göring at the OBERSALZBERG. He usually wears civilian clothes and drives his own Mercedes, in which he willingly gives anyone a lift.

(1) <u>Dr. Karl BRANDT</u> is Plenipotentiary General for Health and Medical Services, holding simultaneous ranks of SS Brigadeführer and General-major der Ordnungspolizei. He is Hitler's doctor in BERLIN and is a rare visitor to the OBERSALZBERG or FHQ, where Dr. MOREL acts as Hitler's physician. BRANDT is 170 cm. in height and slim. Frequently wears the uniform of a Major-general of the Ordnungs-polizei.

(m) <u>Dr. MORELL</u>, Hitler's personal physician at the OBERSALZBERG. Age about 60; corpulent, medium height. with grey hair standing up like a brush.

(n) <u>Gruppenführer TIEFENBACHER</u> is in command of the Begleitkommando.

(o) <u>DÜHRING</u>, Major-domo, at the Berghof, where his wife acts as housekeeper.

(p) <u>Hauptsturmführer MÜLLER of the RSD</u>. Age about 30; height 1.87 m.; dark, short hair, noticeably dark complexion. Formerly in the Waffen SS, whose uniform he wears with a WIKING armband on left cuff.

(q) <u>Obersturmführer UBART</u> in command of the SS Wachkompanie in May 1944.

(r) <u>Sturmbannführer FRANK</u> chief of the SS Kommando OBERSALZBERG. Generally seen in mufti.

(s) <u>Sturmbannführer SPAHN</u> head of the SS Verwachung OBERSALZBERG and is assisted by -

(t) <u>Unterstumführer BREDOW</u> chief of Air Raid Control.

(u) <u>Hauptsturmführer SCHWIEGE</u> commands the smoke unit (Nebelabteilung) at the OBERSALZBERG.

(v) <u>Obersturmführer KREIDERER</u> in charge of the SS Dienstwagenhalle.

(w) <u>Obersturmführer VATER of the SA</u> is responsible for looking after guests visiting the Berghof, assisted by 3 LAH men - WEISS, SCHNEIDER and BUSCHMANN.

(x) <u>Frau SCHAFLYTZEL</u> is Hitler's personal cook at the Berghof.

D. Possibilities of action in the Berchtesgaden area.

In the absence of first-hand information on the OBERSALZBERG since May of this year and in particular since the attentat of July 20th, it is not possible to say whether security and safety measures have been tightened up of late, or whether extra precautions are being taken at FHQ only.

The possibilities of action in the Berchtesgaden area considered below are based on the conditions obtaining there in May 1944.

1. Timing.

The readiest indication of Hitler's presence in the OBERSALZBERG is the big swastika flag which is flown on such occasions from the flagpole at the car park in front of the BERGHOF.[+] Amongst other view-points this flag is visible from the SCHELLENBERG-UNTERAU road (Fig.1), the Cafe ROTTENHOFER (Fig.30), and the DOKTORBERG, both in Berchtesgaden.

Another indication is the presence in the neighbourhood of the various Sonderzüge (special trains), viz. Hitler's at Schloss KLESSHEIM sidings (Fig.61), Keitel's at BISCHOFSWIESEN, the Gästezug (visitors' train) at Berchtesgaden and Ribbentrop's train at Salzburg (Fig.62).

A third clue to Hitler's presence at the OBER-SALZBERG is provided by the clientele of the Wirthaus HOFSCHAFNER (Fig.30) in Berchtesgaden, a tavern much frequented in the evening by members of the SS Führerbegleitkommando when off duty.

2. Suggested course of action.

It is evident from the notes given under C.1.(c) of Hitler's routine that two opportunities present themselves of liquidating the Führer, firstly when on his way to and from the Teehaus on the MOOSLANER KOPF and secondly when en route to or from Schloss KLESSHEIM.

In neither case would the operation be an easy one or without peril, particularly in the former instance, i.e. the MOOSLANER KOPF, for here not only have we to reckon with wire fences but with SS piquets and patrols as well as the RSD dog patrol.

(a) Action at the MOOSLANER KOPF (Fig.2). Action here is nevertheless worthy of consideration in view of the fact that whereas a considerable interval of time may elapse between Hitler's visits to Schloss KLESSHEIM and other FHQs [x] the Führer rarely misses

---

+ P/W informant, ex-SS Wachkompanie Obersalzberg, is emphatic on the existence of this flag and on the fact that it is only flown when Hitler is at the Berghof.

x In 1943 and the earlier part of 1944 (i.e. before the invasion of France and during the lull on the Russian front) Hitler is said to have remained at the Berghof for weeks on end. This is unlikely to be the case nowadays, when his departures from the OBERSALZBERG may well be as frequent as his walks to the MOOSLANER KOPF.

his daily walk to the teahouse on the MOOSLANER KOPF (30 in Fig.2). Thus from the middle of March 1944, before which date the snow was too thick, Hitler went to the Teehaus nearly every day.

Hitler is reported to set out from the Berghof for the Teehaus between 1000 and 1100 hrs. following the route marked in Fig.2. Walking alone, the Führer is under observation throughout his walk by the SS patrol which follows him at a discreet distance. Hitler is also under the observation of the SS piquet at the GUTSHOF for about 1000 yards of the walk, and is visible to the SS piquets at the Theaterhalle and the Landhaus Göring as he crosses the concrete by-pass from the OBERAU road to the Führerstrasse. These piquets are, however, well over 500 yards away.

The modus operandi suggested is as follows:-

(i) <u>Approach</u>: From the LAROSBACH (Fig.2) through the woods to the wire fence near the point at which the concrete by-pass cuts the route followed by Hitler in his walk. The operative or operatives (supposing two snipers are employed) should be in position, (say) between this point and the teahouse, not earlier than 1000 hrs. (to give RSD dog patrol time to have passed). The position taken up should be within 100-200 yards of the route.

(ii) <u>Weapon and equipment</u>: Mauser sniper's rifle, telescopic sight (carried in pocket), explosive bullets in magazine, wire-cutters (for making hole in wire fence), H.E. grenades carried in haversac for close protection and assistance in making get-away.

(iii) <u>Disguise</u>: Gebirgsjäger uniform. The great majority of the patients at the Lazarett (military hospital) in the PLATTERHOF are mountain troops. (Gebirgsjäger). Since the SS Führerbegleit-kommando, the RSD (when not in mufti) and the SS Wach-kompanie Obersalzberg all wear this type of uniform (Fig.35a) in winter (with slight modifications), imper-sonation on these lines would obviously facilitate approach to within striking distance. The modifications converting a Gebirgsjäger uniform into that worn by the SS personnel at the Obersalzberg are very quickly made. They merely consist of moving the Hoheitsabzeichen from above the right breast-pocket to the left sleeve above the elbow; removing the red, white and black rosette and Hoheitsabzeichen from the front of the Bergmütze and substituting for it the Totenkopf (death's head) emblem; changing the Wehrmacht collar patches for the SS flash and badge of rank (worn respectively on the right and left sides of the collar) - as shown in Fig.44, and perhaps removing the Edelweiss from the left side of the cap (Bergmütze).

Bergmütze   Collar patch   Bergmütze   Collar patch   Collar patch
                                          (right side). (left side).

Fig.44a. Gebirgsjäger.   Fig.44b. Unterscharführer of
                               Begleitkommando or SS Wachkompanie.

                                  Illustration also shown in colour p. 166

(iv) <u>Alternative action at the Teehaus</u>. Assuming that the sniper failed and Hitler reached the tea-house unharmed, it might be possible to retrieve the situation, and even to regard the sniper's attempt as a diversion, by attacking Hitler in his car on the return journey to the BERGHOF. This attack would be made by two operatives firing a PIAT gun (or Bazooka) from the woods in the vicinity of the Teehaus. These operatives would not take up position until the arrival of the Kolonne at the Teehaus after observing the sniper's failure to bring down Hitler. They would thus avoid the risk of detection by any piquets and patrols in the neighbourhood of the MOOSLANER KOPF, whose attention would rather be drawn in the opposite direction. The Kolonne, one may reasonably assume, would be sent for post haste following the sniper's attempt. Whether Hitler returned alone to the Berghof or took his breakfast at the teahouse before returning, the guards would hardly expect a second attack to be made.

(b) <u>Action on the BERGHOF-Schloss KLESSHEIM road (Figs.1 and 2)</u>.

(i) <u>Place</u>: The route taken by Hitler when driving to Schloss KLESSHEIM is as follows:-

Out at Post No.1, past the AUERSTRASSE Posten, through OBERAU, UNTERAU, SCHELLENBERG, GRÖDIG, and thence on the Autobahn, circling SALZBURG, and skirting MAXGLAN.

As Fig.1 indicates almost the entire route from the Berghof as far as GRÖDIG is wooded. Except for a stretch of some 500 yards before reaching OBERAU and of about 100 yards on the other side of the village the Führerstrasse is heavily wooded all the way except for a few clearings. For a stretch of a kilometre in the vicinity of UNTERSTEIN the woods are described as particularly thick and come right down to the road.

The stretch of road north of SCHELLENBERG where the Führerstrasse rejoins the Berchtesgaden-Salzburg main road, appears from air-photos to have woods on both sides in close proximity to the road, i.e. between heights 925 and 1189, though the woods in the vicinity of St. LEONHARD-KELLERBRUNN have been cleared.

Adequate cover would therefore be available to a party armed with PIAT guns (or Bazookas) and H.E. and smoke grenades. (for close protection). The point chosen for delivering the attack should not only afford the necessary cover but preferably be situated at a sharp bend in the road which the Kolonne would be forced therefore to take at reduced speed.

(ii) <u>Guarding of route</u>. Until 1940 (at any rate) the road from the Berghof to Salzburg (in those days via the Schiessstandbrücke) was not guarded. More recent information (May 1944) indicate

however, that the route from the Berghof via OBERAU,
UNTERAU, GRÖDIG to Schloss KLESSHEIM (or Salzburg)
is guarded by SS and RSD personnel. No details are
available as to the spacing of sentries along the
route or whether they are only placed at dangerous
points. Intervals between guards (who must in any
case be few in number) must be considerable.

(iii) The Kolonne. Before the war and certainly
until well into 1940 Hitler's Kolonne usually totalled
some 10 cars (see Appendix I), of which Hitler's was
always the leading car. The latter was followed by
4 cars each carrying six SS guards with members of
Hitler's entourage following in the remaining 5 cars.
Since then the Kolonne appears to have been somewhat
reduced in size, though it never consists of less
than three MERCEDES-NÜRBURG 6-seater cars. The
Kolonne is nowadays preceded (contrary to previous
practice) by a RSD man on a motor-cycle or MC
combination, who rides about 200 yards ahead of the
leading car, and is armed with a Machine pistol.
When motoring to Schloss KLESSHEIM Hitler usually
rides inthe second car and always in front[+] alongside his chauffeur Obersturmführer KEMKA (Fig.),
with Eva BRAUN and/or Brigadeführer RATTENHUBER of
the RSD in the back of the car. He drives very
fast in order to minimise the chance of being hit.
The readiest means of recognising the car is by the
pennant on the right-hand front mudguard (see
Appendix I).

If instead of taking the Führerzug at the
KLESSHEIM sidings Hitler takes the train at Berchtesgaden, the route followed will be the Führerstrasse
to the SCHIESSSTANDBRÜCKE (Figs.1 and 30) over the
R. ACHE and thence to the station at Berchtesgaden
(Fig.30), a route which likewise passes through well-
wooded country affording good cover. In this case,
however, the road is a good deal shorter than that
to Schloss KLESSHEIM and therefore easier to guard.

(iv) Timing of the attack. The question of
timing is considerably more difficult than in the
case of the MOOSLANER KOPF. It would be necessary
to keep the car-park in front of the Berghof under
constant observation from 1000 hrs. onwards. This
car-park is visible from the SCHELLENBERG-UNTERAU
road. The numerous empty huts in the UNTERAU
district might furnish usefull hideouts.

According to recent press reports Hitler has
taken up his quarters in the Führerzug, which for
safety is run into a tunnel. Attached as he is to
the OBERSALZBERG Hitler is likely to continue to
snatch as much time as he can there. The nearest
tunnel to the Berghof is the one on the Berchtesgaden - Bad Reichenhall line (Fig.1) - apart from
the tunnel reported to have been built under the
Bavaria (Fig.30).

+ Hitler only rides in the back on ceremonial occasions,
  e.g. visits of foreign notabilities, Mussolini, for example.

In the event of Hitler spending his time between
these tunnels and the BERGHOF (where deep air raid
shelters exist), the Führerstrasse between Obersalzberg and Berchtesgaden would be the scene of the
attack. Hideouts for the PIAT party might in this
case be found in the empty huts on the Hoch Lenzer
(Fig.1).

(v) Disguise. This would be the same as that
mentioned above under D 2a (iii). In this case the
operatives might pass themselves off as members of
the Nebelabteilung (smoke unit) who are distributed
in pairs over the whole Obersalzberg area.

3. Combined operation.

Assuming that it would be possible to learn
some hours ahead of Hitler's presence at the
OBERSALZBERG, a combined operation in the form of
an aerial bombardment of the Berghof and the SS
barracks accompanied by the dropping of a paratroop
battalion (S.A.S.) whould be well worth while since
it offers the best chance of eliminating the Führer
as well as other leading Nazis in the OBERSALZBERG,
Martin BORMANN, for instance.

Apart from the Wachkompanie, the Begleitkommando
and the RSD with a total of about 260-280 all ranks,
there would be little opposition, since the smoke
and A.A. personnel are scattered over a very wide
area. Most of the Begleitkommando and the RSD would
moreover take to the air raid shelters in all
probability, so that the Wachkompanie need alone be
reckoned with. Opposition would, in fact, only be
offered by the men standin-by for duty (Bereitschaft),
the fire-fighting platoon, the piquets over the air
raid shelters and patrols, and the residue of the
Wachkompanie specifically told off for anti-paratroop
duties. Apart from rifles, machine pistols, the
armament of the Wachkompanie consists only of 12 Mg.,
2 old 8 cm. mortars and a few 5 cm. mortars. A
paratroop battalion could therefore swamp any resistance the troops guarding the OBERSALZBERG might put
up.

Nor would it be possible for the garrisons of
Salzburg and BAD REICHENHALL, assuming they still
exist and have not already been sent to man the
Western defences, to send help in time. Aerial
bombardment could, in any case, be extended to
Salzburg and Bad Reichenhall following the attack
on the BERGHOF.

It was hoped at one time that this operation
might be planned to take place in conjunction with
a revolt by the foreign workers of the Salzburg
area, in particular by French deportees and Ps/W,
and Poles and Ostarbeiter, whose first action would
have been to seize the arms depots in the Salzburg
area marked 1,2,3, and 4 in Fig.1. There appears, however,
little possibility of cooperation at the present
time with the foreign governments in this connection.

Such information as is available on foreign
workers in the Salzburg and Berchtesgaden areas is
included in Appendix III.

Part II. THE FÜHRERZUG AS THE SCENE OF ACTION.

A. The Führerzug.

1. General Description.

Originally presented to the Führer by a group of industrial magnates, the train has been used by Hitler, not only on official visits to the heads of other Fascist governments, e.g. Mussolini and Franco, but also as a mobile headquarters when visiting the various theatres of war.

The Führerzug may be distinguished from the other special trains (Sonderzüge) used by Ribbentrop, Keitel, and Himmler, for example, by its colour, which is described nowadays as a dirty violet or very dark blue (approaching black). Until recently its colour was darkish green like that of the other Sonderzüge. + It is streamlined and appears to be lower than the normal German train. The chief features which distinguish the Sonderzüge (and the Führerzug) from ordinary Reichsbahn or Mitropa rolling stock are their larger windows, wider concertina gangways between coaches, their superior coachwork, the 1½ ins. white stripe under the windows and at the bottom of the panelling along the whole length of the train (see Figs.47 and 48), and the telephone connections between coaches. x

It has been said, and the statement has been confirmed, that the Führerzug is sometimes divided into three parts, viz. an advance train (Vorzug) with the code name KLEINASIEN, a main train (in which Hitler nearly always travels) with the code name AMERIKA, and a rear train (Nachzug) with ASIEN as its code name. No information is available regarding distance and/or time between parts, though on one occasion the main train (Hauptzug) is said to have left SALZBURG 1½ hrs. (0930 hrs.) after the Vorzug (0800 hrs.). Informant has stated that the main train can be distinguished from the other two (at close quarters) by the telephone wires from the two locomotives which link up with the train as far back as the W/T coach, and by the disruptive pattern painted on the roofs of the coaches as camouflage. Another distinguishing feature is that only the part in which Hitler travels is believed to have a saloon coach. It is not unlikely that the three trains are only used on special occasions. They are, for example, said to have been repainted (dark green) at POTSDAM during the spring of 1942, prior to Hitler's journey to HENDAYE to meet Franco. The first train is described as carrying various members of Hitler's staff, with Hitler and his immediate entourage, including the Begleitkommando in the second train and security police in the third.

+ Though a reliable source describes Göring's special as a dirty violet in colour.

x. These are described as only visible between coaches and even then as difficult to see.

Another informant who was one of Hitler's body-servants (Bursch) until mid-1940 and frequently travelled on the train denies the existence of duplicate Führerzüge. Nor were the latter met with on the Eastern Front (Polish Corridor) during the Russian campaign (see Appendix IV below). The nearest approach to anything of the kind is the advance train, which, according to three Austrian railwaymen well acquainted with Sonderzug procedure, always precedes, in Germany at any rate, every Sonderzug. This advance train consists of a locomotive with one or two coaches carrying railway police (Bahnpolizei) who are set down to reinforce the local railway police when necessary.

2. Composition of the Führerzug.

Disregarding any question of advance, main and rear parts, the Führerzug as used by Hitler to travel between Freilassing, Salzburg (Berchtesgaden, Schloss Klessheim railhead) and the various FHQs consists of two locomotives and some 14 coaches.[+] The composition of the train in 1940 is given as follows:-

No. of coach from front to rear.	Description.
1.	Forward Flak (A.A.) coach.
2,3.	Begleitkommando.
4.	Dienstpersonal (train staff).
5.	Telephone and W/T coach.
6.	Secretariat.
7.	Bormann and his staff.
8.	Dining car and kitchen (Mitropa).
9.	Adjutants.
10.	Hitler's saloon coach.
11,12,13.	Various high personages.
14.	Rear Flak (A.A.) coach.

Another (later) report describes the Führerzug as consisting, in 1943 (during the Russian campaign), of two locomotives and 10-11 coaches. In this case the sequence from first to rear is given as follows:-

Coach with armoured cupola mounting tank gun or MG
Flak (A.A.) coach mounting quadruple (Vierling) A.gun
6-7 coaches of the Pullman type
Flak (A.A.) coach with quadruple A.A. gun, and another coach with armoured cupola mounting tank gun or MG.

In 1941 the Führerzug at Schloss Klessheim sidings was described as consisting of about 20 coaches. In neither of the examples given are luggage vans included (unless certain of the coaches incorporated luggage compartments) and it is possible that the Führerzug, like Ribbentrop's special train, has luggage vans at either end of the train.

+ Figures given vary from 6 to 9-10 and even 20 coaches.

The coach marked **Dienstpersonal** is probably
a Salonpackwagen as on Ribbentrop's train. Comparing
the two trains the chief difference is the inclusion
of two dining cars on Ribbentrop's train, though part
of one, it is true, is used as the Secretariat. The
Secretariat coach on Hitler's train may therefore be
of the same type (see Fig. 56). The position of the
W/T coach on Hitler's train is not known for certain
and it has been placed in front of the Secretariat
coach as the most likely place. In Ribbentrop's
train of 14 coaches it is the eighth car from the
front. Not only coaches 11. 12. and 13. but Bormann's
coach may on occasion drop out, so that the figure of
9-10 coaches given for Hitler's train may therefore
be correct at times.

Fig.45 shows the Führerzug entering the Anhalter
Bahnhof, Berlin, on Hitler's return from France in
1940, and gives some idea of the length of the train
with its two locomotives.

Fig.45. The Führerzug entering the Anhalter Bahnhof
on the occasion of Hitler's return to Berlin after
the Battle of France.

This photograph gives some idea of the length of the
train with its two locomotives.

Fig.46 shows a view of part of the train at
SUBOTICA, 1941, on the occasion of Hitler's 52nd
birthday, whilst Figs.47 and 48 give a close up
view of the coaches and the white stripe below the
windows and at the base of the panelling. This is
also visible in Fig.49, which shows Hitler leaning
out of the window of his saloon coach. Fig.50 shows
one of the locomotives which, as Figs.51 and 52
indicate, is followed immediately by the A.A. coach.

-73-

80

Fig.46. The Führerzug at SUBOTICA (20th April 1941) on the occasion of Hitler's
52nd birthday.

117

81

KEITEL   RAEDER   HITLER BRAUCHITSCH   GÖRING.

Fig.47. Führer's coach at SUBOTIC. (20th April 1941).

118

82

Brigadeführer ALBRECHT.

Fig.48. Another view of the Führer's coach (Subotica – 20th April 1941).

Fig.49. Hitler leaning out of the window of his Salonwagen.

Note: The distinguishing white stripe below window along whole length of coach and at bottom of panelling, characteristic of all special trains including the Führerzug. Painted darkest green like all Sonderzüge, the colour of the Führer's train is now reported to have been altered to dark blue or violet.

120

Fig.50. Locomotive of Führerzug (Anhalter Bahnhof,
Berlin, July 1940).

Fig.51. Locomotives and Flakwagen (A.A. coach) of the
Führerzug (Anhalter Bahnhof, Berlin, July 1940).

Fig. 52. Flakwagen (A.A. coach) of the Führerzug
(Anhalter Bahnhof, Berlin, July 1940).

3. <u>The coaches of the Führerzug</u>.

The internal layout of certain of the coaches
on the Führerzug is described below, and shown in
Figs. 53-58.

(a) <u>The A.A. coaches.</u> The layout of each of the A.A. coaches (on Ribbentrop's train) is shown in Fig.53 below. It is believed to be identical with that of the Flakwagen on Hitler's train.

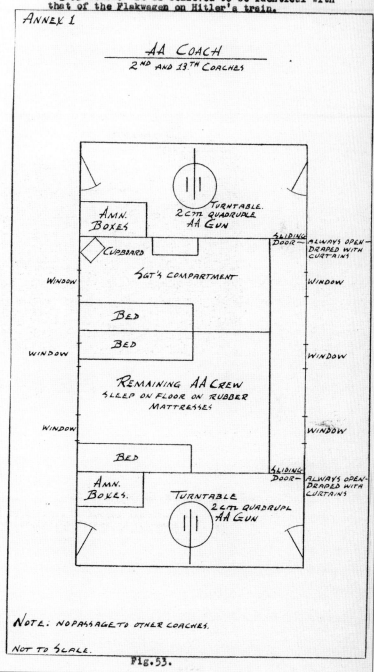

ANNEX 1

AA COACH
2ND AND 13TH COACHES

NOTE: NO PASSAGE TO OTHER COACHES.

NOT TO SCALE.

Fig.53.

(b) **Salonpackwagen**. (Dienstpersonalwagen). The
layout of this coach is shown in Fig.54 below.

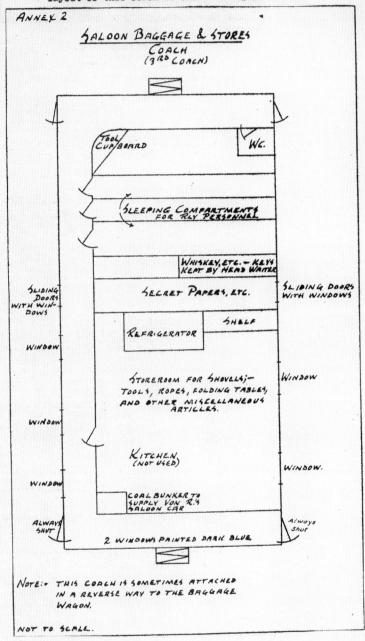

ANNEX 2

SALOON BAGGAGE & STORES
COACH
(3RD COACH)

TOOL CUPBOARD

W.C.

SLEEPING COMPARTMENTS
FOR RLY PERSONNEL

WHISKEY, ETC. - KEYS
KEPT BY HEAD WAITER

SLIDING DOORS
WITH WINDOWS

SECRET PAPERS, ETC.

SLIDING DOORS
WITH WINDOWS

WINDOW

REFRIGERATOR   SHELF

STOREROOM FOR SHOVELS;-
TOOLS, ROPES, FOLDING TABLES,
AND OTHER MISCELLANEOUS
ARTICLES.

WINDOW

WINDOW

KITCHEN
(NOT USED)

WINDOW.

WINDOW

COAL BUNKER TO
SUPPLY VON R.'S
SALOON CAR

ALWAYS
SHUT

Always
Shut

2 WINDOWS PAINTED DARK BLUE

NOTE:- THIS COACH IS SOMETIMES ATTACHED
IN A REVERSE WAY TO THE BAGGAGE
WAGON.

NOT TO SCALE.

Fig.54.

124

(c) The W/T coach. The interior of the W/T coach
on Ribbentrop's train is shown in Fig.55. On the
assumption that this is standard for all Sonderzüge,
the one on Hitler's train will have the same layout.

ANNEX 7

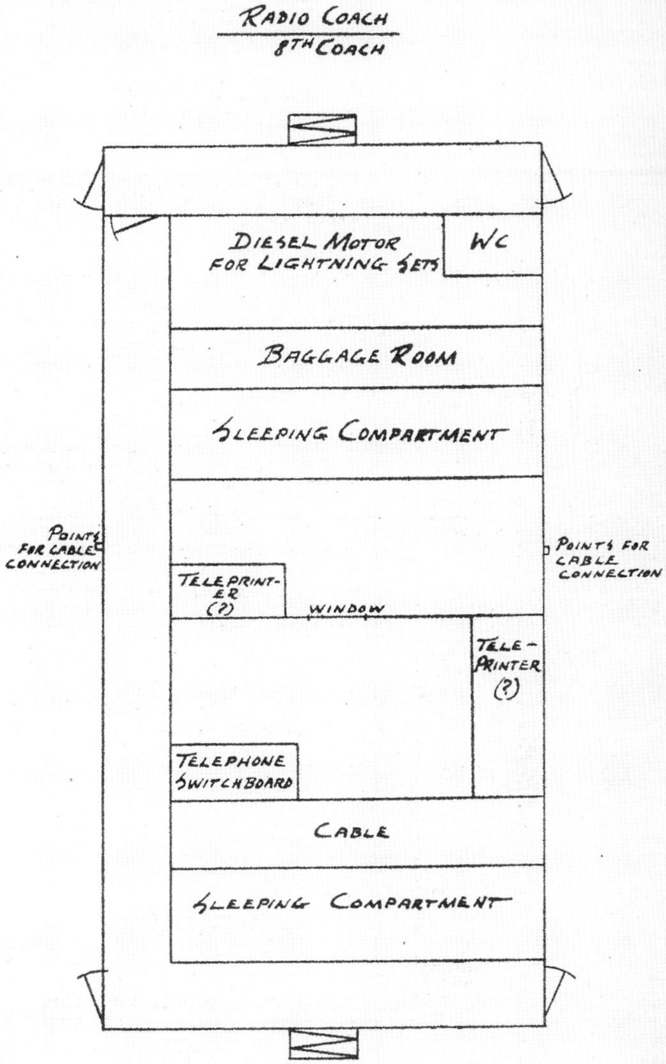

RADIO COACH

8TH COACH

DIESEL MOTOR
FOR LIGHTNING SETS

WC

BAGGAGE ROOM

SLEEPING COMPARTMENT

POINTS
FOR CABLE
CONNECTION

POINTS FOR
CABLE
CONNECTION

TELE PRINT-
ER
(?)

WINDOW

TELE-
PRINTER
(?)

TELEPHONE
SWITCHBOARD

CABLE

SLEEPING COMPARTMENT

NOT TO SCALE.

Fig.55.

89

(d) <u>Sekretariatwagen</u>. On Ribbentrop's special train
this coach is a converted Mitropa dining car, and it
is not unlikely that much the same arrangement has
been adopted on Hitler's train for accommodating the
Führer's secretaries. The layout of this coach is
shown in Fig.56 below.

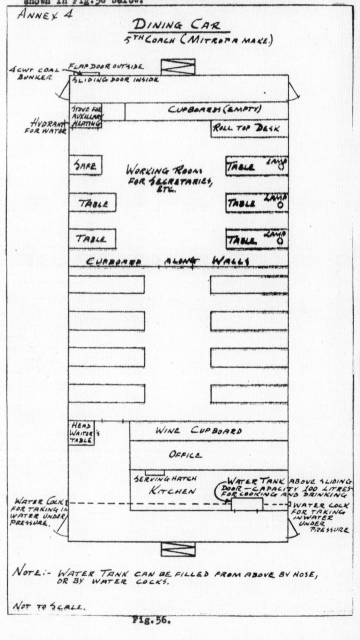

ANNEX 4

DINING CAR
5TH COACH (MITROPA MAKE.)

4 CWT COAL BUNKER. FLAP DOOR OUTSIDE
SLIDING DOOR INSIDE

STOVE FOR AUXILIARY HEATING
CUPBOARDS (EMPTY)

HYDRANT FOR WATER
ROLL TOP DESK

SAFE
WORKING ROOM FOR SECRETARIES, ETC.
TABLE — LAMP

TABLE
TABLE — LAMP

TABLE
TABLE — LAMP

CUPBOARD ALONG WALLS

HEAD WAITER'S TABLE
WINE CUPBOARD

OFFICE

SERVING HATCH
KITCHEN
WATER TANK ABOVE SLIDING DOOR — CAPACITY 100 LITRES FOR COOKING AND DRINKING

WATER COCK FOR TAKING IN WATER UNDER PRESSURE.
WATER COCK FOR TAKING IN WATER UNDER PRESSURE

NOTE:- WATER TANK CAN BE FILLED FROM ABOVE BY HOSE, OR BY WATER COCKS.

NOT TO SCALE.

Fig. 56.

90

(e) <u>The dining car</u>. Assuming this to be of
same type as in Ribbentrop's train, the layo
be that depicted in Fig.57.

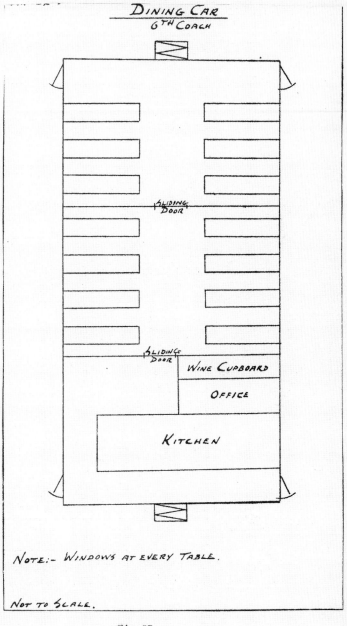

DINING CAR
6TH COACH

SLIDING DOOR

SLIDING DOOR

WINE CUPBOARD

OFFICE

KITCHEN

NOTE:- WINDOWS AT EVERY TABLE.

NOT TO SCALE.

Fig.57.

(f) <u>Hitler's Salonwagen</u>. The internal arrangement of
this coach (in 1940) was that shown below in Fig.58.
The bed itself is said to be of the tip-up type.

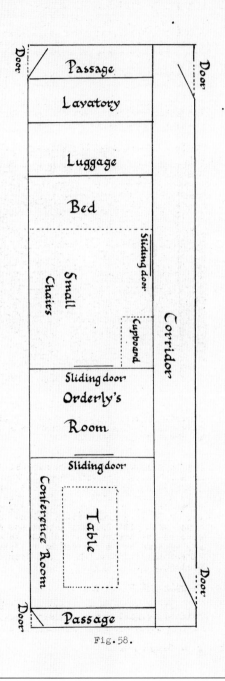

Fig.58.

B. Protection of the Führerzug.

1. Protection on the train itself.

(a) <u>En route</u>. The Begleitkommando on the train is about 20 strong, of whom two-thirds are SS Leibstandarte personnel and the remainder Sipo/SD (Gestapo)+ men. Two men are always on duty at the entrances at either end of Hitler's coach. At stops the Begleitkommando descends and forms a bodyguard round Hitler, never leaving his side. (see Fig.59).

The total strength of the train personnel, including Flak and Begleitkommando, waiters, and railway employees is 100-120.

Fig.59. Hitler leaving the Anhalter Bahnhof on his return to Berlin from France (July 1940) followed by the Begleitkommando.

(b) <u>In the sidings</u>. (FREILASSING, Schloss KLESSHEIM, or SALZBURG). The only details available on the guarding of Sonderzüge are those applying to RIBBENTROP's special train. In this case four of the Flak personnel are on guard during daylight; at night the train is guarded (at SALZBURG) by two Bahnpolizei armed with pistols, who patrol the line on either side of the train. When Hitler is at FHQ the Führerzug appears to be guarded by a detachment from the Führerbegleitbataillon of the Grossdeutschland Division.

2. Guarding of the route.

This includes stations and track (tunnels, bridges, signal boxes, points, etc.).

+ Frequently wearing mufti.

(a) <u>Stations</u>. According to four out of five
informants, platforms are not usually cleared of
civilians either by day or by night, when a Sonderzug stops or passes through the station, nor are
special guards mounted on stations through which
Sonderzüge run non-stop (in this case the train is
stated usually to go through on a line not adjacent
to the platform). According to one informant a
certain number of railway police, train and local
Gestapo (some in mufti) are, however, always on
guard when the train stops. These men walk up and
down the platform at which the train is standing,
Bahnpolizei being also stationed on the remoter
platforms. The only restriction laid on civilians,
according to another informant, is that the police
try to clear the public back on the platforms (as
shown in Fig.60), but when the train stops, the
crowd throngs right up to the coach to try to touch
the Führer (as shown in Fig.49). This information,
it is true, dates from 1940, when Hitler was in his
heyday, and it is possible that safety measures
have been tightened up of late, and that the Bahnpolizei now allow no-one near the train; they are
also said to see that railway employees servicing
the train do not loiter unnecessarily.

Stops at stations are said to last as long as
half an hour.

Fig.60.

(b) <u>Track</u>. In Russia, as in other occupied territories,
it has been the practice to guard the line heavily
with Bahnpolizei (and if required troops), with
sentries every 100-200 m. during the passing of a
Sonderzug. This has not, at any rate until recently,
been the practice in Germany, though the rails may
be inspected by a Reichsbahn official.

The guarding of the railways in Austria appears to be slacker than elsewhere in the Reich. Signal boxes are not guarded as a rule, bridges and tunnels are guarded by the military, and stations by the Bahnpolizei.[+] Guards at bridges and tunnels are said to consist of only two men and to be very slack in performing their duties.

The guarding of railways in occupied territory in the early stages of the war (1941), according to the account of an attempt by a Polish resistance group to blow up Hitler's train in West Prussia (Polish Corridor) given in Appendix IV, was also carried out by Bahnpolizei. The latter are stated to have patrolled the line from time to time, but to have spent most of the time near the points and signal boxes, (the latter being quite close to the points they operate). The Bahnpolizei normally carried out single patrols and were armed with rifles and hand grenades. Signal boxes were always too strongly guarded for any attempt to be made on them.

The bridges and stations were usually patrolled, but broadly speaking, there was little supervision in open country; patrols along the line were always made before Hitler's train was expected. In spite of these precautions this particular resistance group all but succeeded in their object.

(c) Warning system. A special time-table is made out for Sonderzüge and circulated by the Bahndirektion to the stations concerned via the Zugleitungen. This information is passed telegraphically. Information regarding the route and timing of Sonderzüge is stated to be in the possession of the Zugleitungen (Train Control) 12-24 hours ahead and of the minor stations about 30 mins. in advance.[x] The arrival of special trains is apparently announced by number only.

In regard to Hitler's train, the Zugleitungen and stations concerned are warned of the arrival of the train perhaps 3-4 hours ahead, others concerned only knowing about 20 mins. in advance. Sometimes the arrival of the Sonderzug is disguised by the announcement that it is a goods train, for instance, which is passing through. The arrival of Sonderzüge is stated by one informant to have been known to the local inhabitants of SALZBURG well in advance, possibly as a result of careless talk on the part of

---

[+] Railway police are normally armed with revolvers (sometimes with rifles or machine pistols). Uniforms are grey-green, army pattern, with a cog wheel on the black collar patch. Shoulder straps are of green and white intertwined cords, and also bear a cog wheel.

[x] At AMSTETTEN (AUSTRIA) for example, the railway officials were informed verbally some hours in advance that the special train was expected, though the full details did not arrive until 20 mins. before the train was due (Russians, French and Polish are employed on the railway at AMSTETTEN).

officials on the local Gauleiter's staff or perhaps
the train staff.[+]

Lines are cleared for Sonderzüge only to the
extent that the special train is not held up; in
the case of Hitler's train all traffic, it has been
said, is brought to a standstill and no shunting is
allowed while the train is passing.

The railway staff responsible for supervising
the passage of special trains is the Betriebswerk-
vorstand and the Amtsvorstand.

C. Servicing of Special Trains.

Servicing is here taken as including washing
and provisioning.

1. Washing.

Coaches of von RIBBENTROP's train are washed
outside SALZBURG station by half a dozen French
women, the final wash being carried out the day
before the train is due to leave. The interior is
cleaned by Reichsbahn employees. The siding at which
this operation is performed is shown in Fig.62. The
Führerzug is usually serviced at Schloss KLESSHEIM by
Führerbegleitbataillon personnel, though it has
recently been seen on von Ribbentrop's siding at
Salzburg, alongside GÖRING's train.

2. Provisioning.

(a) Water for drinking and cooking purposes is taken
on at station stops en route between rail hydrants,
the hose from the hydrant being either connected up
from the fresh-water tank on the roof of the dining
car (see Fig.64) or from water cocks on either side
of the coach. The former procedure is adopted when
there is not sufficient pressure behind the water
supply.

When in the sidings at Salzburg, von Ribbentrop's
train is shunted about 12 noon daily for this purpose
from the main siding to a goods siding. Each coach is
brought in turn past the hydrant between the rails,
after which the train is taken back to the siding.
The routine intake of water occupies about one hour.
Similar hydrants are available at FREILASSING junction
for the Führerzug when Salzburg is not used for the
purpose of taking in water.

[+] The following places of refreshment in Salzburg are frequented
by train personnel (sleeping car attendants, waiters, engine
drivers): Cafe BURGUND, the PITTER Cafe (on the first floor
of the PITTER Hotel), the PITTERBRÄUSTUBL, and the Cafe MOZART
in the Getreidegasse. This latter is also patronised by
Führerbegleitbataillon personnel from Schloss KLESSHEIM, who
also frequent the WALCHER MÜHLE in the MAXGLAN suburb of Salzburg. Places frequented by the SS Wachkompanie Obersalzberg in
Salzburg include the MIRABELLE KASINO, the PLATZLKELLER, the
ZUR TRAUBE, the GLOCKENSPIEL and the Cafe LOHR. The PITTER-
KELLER is frequented by Bahnpolizei. The French women respon
sible for washing v. Ribbentrop's train at Salzburg station a
often to be found in the evening (after 5 p.m.) at the MOZART
or PITTER Cafes or at the Cafe FÜNFHAUS, although they have
be back at their Lager (camp) by 10 or 11 p.m. (They can b'
"dated").

(b) Other supplies. Beer, mineral waters, chocolate, malt and coffee used to be taken aboard at the Anhalter Bahnhof, sufficient quantities being delivered to last for 4-6 weeks. Potatoes and other vegetables as well as meat and fruit are usually delivered to the train at Salzburg.

All food and drink on the Führerzug are kept in the kitchen (cupboards). KANNENBERG, the Intendant at the Reichskanzlei is responsible for ordering food for the train in BERLIN and MUNICH. In BERLIN it used to be delivered by MITROPA though Hitler's food was specially brought from the Reichskanzlei in BERLIN or from the Berghof.

D. Routeing of the Führerzug.

Two routes are considered below, viz. to the north and to the west.

1. To the north (BERLIN).

The route followed by the Führerzug in travelling from BERCHTESGADEN or Schloss KLESSHEIM is as follows:-

BERCHTESGADEN
BAD REICHENHALL   or   Schloss KLESSHEIM

FREILASSING Junction

MÜHLDORF

LANDSHUT   or   MUNICH

PLAUEN

or

LEIPZIG   HALLE

BERLIN
(Anhalter Bahnhof).

Stops are made at LANDSHUT, REGENSBURG, HOF, LEIPZIG or HALLE (more often the latter). Special trains may also stop at JÜTERBOG or LÜCKENWALDE where Hitler, Himmler, Ribbentrop etc. with their entourages may leave the train and complete the journey by car to BERLIN. Neither the Führerzug nor von Ribbentrop's special stops at FREILASSING Junction. The speed of the Führerzug varies from 90-120 kilometres p.h., 100 km. p.h. being the average maximum.

On the journey from BERLIN to SALZBURG the two steam locomotives are changed for electric locomotives at HALLE. During the winter months, however, one electric and one steam locomotive are used instead of two electric locomotives. The locomotives are changed again either at RODENKIRCHEN or at PROSTZELLA and again at NUREMBERG or REGENSBURG. A further change may also be made at LANDSHUT. The only tunnel on this route is the short tunnel 2.7 km. north of ROHRBACH, disregarding the tunnel just outside BERCHTESGADEN.

2. **To the west.** (MANNHEIM).

    The route after passing through FREILASSING
Junction followed by the Führerzug in this case is
believed to be as follows: MUNICH, AUGSBURG, ULM,
STUTTGART, HEIDELBERG, MANNHEIM.   The track is
electric as far as Stuttgart.

    The only tunnels on this line are at Stuttgart,
viz. one tunnel 340 m. long in the BAD CANSTATT-
STUTTGARTER HAUPTBAHNHOF section (actually in the
town) and another 700 m. long between STUTTGART-
NORD and STUTTGART-Feuerbach on the other side of
the town.

E. **Possibilities of action in connection with the Führerzug.**

    It is evident from the foregoing notes that the
information available regarding the Führerzug and
its movements is nothing like so complete or precise
as the information given for the Berchtesgaden projects
(in Part I).   The expediency of a final check-up on
the spot by the operatives or their leader before
carrying out the selected project in this case is
stressed.

    The following two addresses in the Salzburg
district might prove useful hide-outs (being places
at which one can stay and no questions asked):
Gasthof MEYER at HOF (a small township 8 miles east
of Salzburg) and Ainringsweg 13, Salzburg-GNEIS 2.

    Actions in connection with the Führerzug are
outlined below.

1. **At the Schloss KLESSHEIM sidings.**

    Fig.1 and Fig.61 (below) show the route from
the Berghof via Schloss Klessheim to the sidings
and the immediate approaches to these sidings.   It
is not known which route the Kolonne takes after
leaving or passing the Schloss.

    If the left-hand fork is taken, the road runs
into the sidings alongside the wood north of the
Schloss.   Though apparently thick enough in summer,
this wood might not afford a great deal of cover in
winter, since its trees are mostly of the deciduous
type.   It should nevertheless afford adequate cover
for a sniper or a PIAT party located at the edge of
the wood (and road) opposite the building at the
N.W. end of the sidings, as well as a good shot
(under 100 yards) at Hitler as he descended from
his car.

    Should the Kolonne take the right-hand fork,
or proceed direct along the Autobahn without touching
Schloss Klessheim, the point at which Hitler would
probably leave his car is in the vicinity of the
building at the S.E. end of the sidings - a distance
of well over 300 yards from the wood and accordingly
out of sniper's range, though probably within range
of a PIAT gun.

    It is true that the wood is uncomfortably close
to Schloss Klessheim and the Führerbegleitbataillon.

The sidings.   Autobahn.

Wood
north
of the
Schloss.

The
Schloss.

Siezenheim.

Fig.61.   Schloss Klessheim and its sidings.

Any attempt as outlined under 2. below to
interfere with the train at the Klessheim sidings
would be out of the question since apart from the
fact that Klessheim is a private station and not open
to the public, the train is guarded and serviced[+]
(washed) by personnel of the Begleitbataillon.

2. At Salzburg railway station.

Fig.62 and 63 show the station and sidings at
Salzburg. Hitler's train is still, it is believed,
occasionally serviced at Salzburg station where it
was reported in July 1944 as occupying the position
shown in Fig.62 (alongside v. Ribbentrop's train).

Only the sides of the coaches of special trains
are washed; the tops of the coaches, it would appear,
are not cleaned. This job is performed by 6 French
workers (female) dressed in black overalls (knee
length, buttoned) without distinguishing badge.
Interference with the drinking and cooking water is
the only clandestine means which offers itself. The
only point at which the water can be "doctored" is
the tank above the kitchen of the MITROPA dining car,
since it appears quite definite that water trolley
wagons are not used (as in this country) for taking
on drinking water

Whether or not it would be possible for one
of these cleaners to get at the tank immediately
above the kitchen of the MITROPA dining car (Fig.64)
during the final wash that special trains are given
shortly before proceeding on a journey is doubtful.
They are apparently approachable (see C. above) and
an attempt to suborn one of them might be worth while.

It might be possible for an operative to introduce the medium at night,[x] provided the guards, as
in the case of v. Ribbentrop's train, consisted of
only a couple of Bahnpolizei, specially if the latter's
attention could be diverted for the necessary time
by a second operative. (The lighting at Salzburg
station is described as extremely poor).

The medium which is described in Appendix V
would best be introduced into the tank in the form
of a strong solution which the jolting of the train
as soon as it got into motion would tend to distribute
evenly in the water.

The capacity of the tank in question is 540 litres,
i.e. about 120 gallons. The quantity of medium necessary
to obtain the desired results is about 768 grams. and
would weigh somewhat under 2 lbs.

+ It is not known whether water for drinking and cooking purposes
can be taken in at the Klessheim sidings or whether the train
has to be taken to Salzburg for this purpose.

x The night before the train was due to leave.

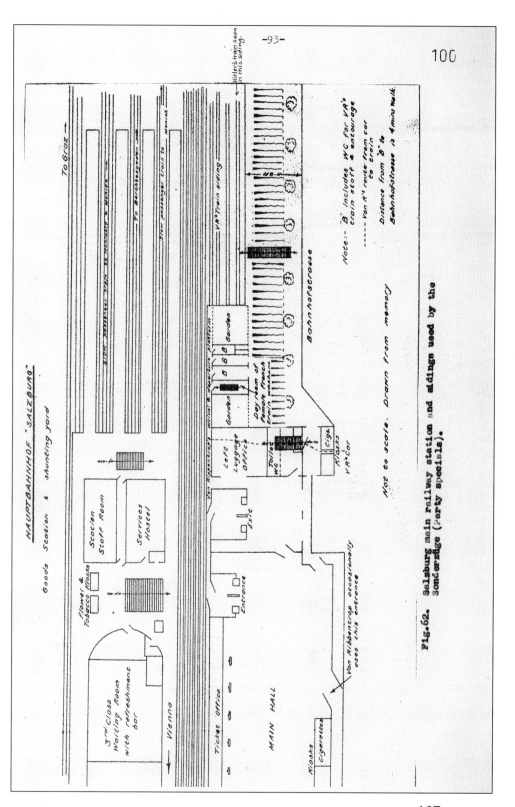

Fig.62. Salzburg main railway station and sidings used by the Sonderzüge (Party specials).

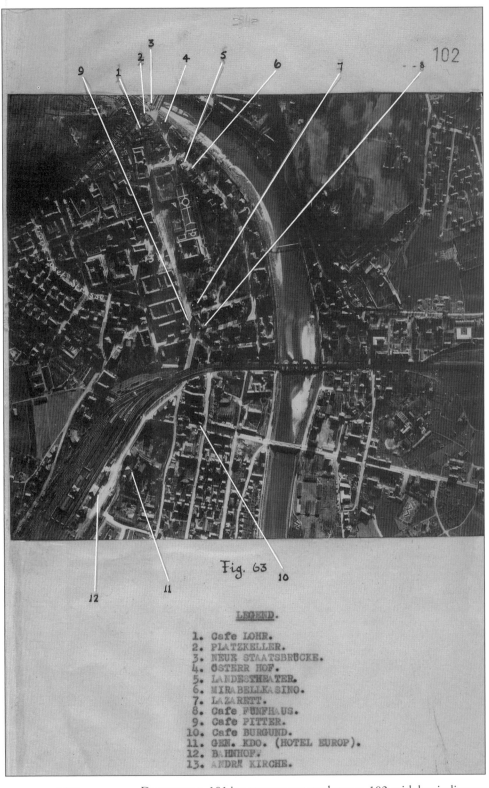

LEGEND.

1. Cafe LOHR.
2. PLATZKELLER.
3. NEUE STAATSBRÜCKE.
4. ÖSTERR HOF.
5. LANDESTHEATER.
6. MIRABELLKASINO.
7. LAZARETT.
8. Cafe FÜNFHAUS.
9. Cafe PITTER.
10. Cafe BURGUND.
11. GEN. KDO. (HOTEL EUROP).
12. BAHNHOF.
13. ANDRÄ KIRCHE.

138   Document p. 101 is a transparent overlay to p. 102, with key indicators

Kitchen.

Fig. 64. MITROPA dining car similar to that used on the Führerzug and the Party specials.

Note: The tank for drinking and cooking water is housed above the kitchen.

3. En route.

From the notes given under B.2 (Protection of the Führerzug) above, the most favourable point for derailing and destroying Hitler's train is a tunnel.[+] In Germany not only is the track itself relatively free from Bahnpolizei or military patrols compared with occupied territory where guards are stationed in some cases every 100-200 yards (as was the case in the Ukraine, for example), but neither bridges nor tunnels are so heavily guarded as in occupied territory (see Fig.65).

Moreover now that every active man is serving at the front, the category of Landesschützen personnel (never very high) is likely in future to be even lower than before. A sabotage party disguised as Bahnpolizei with one member in mufti (as Gestapo man), or as Landesschützen would not arouse the suspicion of the guards, and should be able to "take over", lay their charges as shown in Appendix IV and destroy the train in the tunnel.

Another means of approach in laying charges in longer tunnels, as at Stuttgart for example, would be to enter the tunnel by the ventilation shaft, though this might involve cutting through the ventilation grating (with a blow lamp).

In either case it would be necessary to have an operative (with W/T set) further up the line on which the Führerzug was passing, in order to warn the sabotage party of the train's approach.

An attempt might also be made to derail the train as it passed through a station, by throwing under its wheels a suitcase filled with explosive. For this the train would have to be passing on a track adjacent to the platform on which the operative was standing or only one track removed therefrom, and the operative be prepared to take the consequences.

It is probable that suitable operatives for either of the schemes outlined above would be available among German or Austrian Ps/W. with a sufficiently strong hatred for Hitler.

[+] Should it be found on closer investigation that signal boxes on routes taken by the Führerzug in Germany are only lightly guarded, then the same means (impersonation) as that described for tunnels might be employed here too.

Derailment of Hitler's train when travelling at speed by switching it into a siding, say, has the advantage of requiring no explosion charges.

Landes-
fchützen
halten Wacht

Fig.65.

September. 1944

APPENDIX I - Hitler's Cars.

The cars in which Hitler is driven are always of Mercedes make. No photograph is available of the latest armoured 6 - seater Mercedes-Nürburg type reported to have windscreens and sidescreens of bullet-proof glass 2 ins. thick. They are, however, otherside similar to the Mercedes 4 or 6 wheeled touring cars shown in Figs.67-73 and Figs.76-78 below.

The black Mercedes limousine shown in Figs.74 and 75 is, however, employed in very cold weather, and Hitler is reported to have made considerable use of this type of car in Russia.

Number plates are useless as a means of identifying the Führer's car, the Nationalstandard (Fig.66) carried on the right-hand mudguard + being the surest means of identification: As the photographs show, it is Hitler's practice to sit beside his driver (Sturmbannführer KEMKA) in the leading car, unless accompanied by any important foreign personages like Mussolini or the Regent HORTHY (see Fig.77) when he sits in the back seat.

Hitler's car is however usually the second car in the Kolonne when driving from the Berghof to Schloss Klessheim sidings.

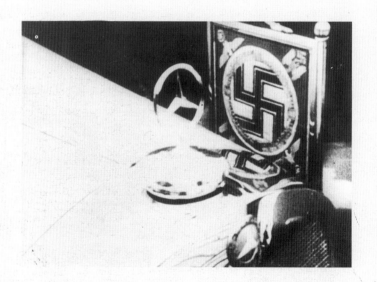

Fig.66.

+ Fig.66 shows it on the left-hand mudguard. This particular photo was taken of Mussolini's car, which bore on the right-hand mudguard the Fascist emblem (lictor's rods).

Fig.67. Hitler at the opening of the Nazi Party Congress, Nuremburg.

Sturmbannführer KEMKA, Hitler's driver, is seated at the Führer's side.

Fig.68. Hitler at Memel.
The seated figure immediately behind Hitler is KRAUSE, once Hitler's valet, and now an officer of the Begleitkommando.

Fig. 69. Hitler at Nuremberg Rally.

Behind Hitler (to his right) KRAUSE and (to his left)
Brigadeführer SCHAUB.

Fig.70. Another photograph of Hitler in his car (Nuremberg Rally).

KRAUSE   ENGELS (a German Wehrmacht (Heer) adjutant)

SCHMUNDT

Fig.71. Hitler in 6-wheeled Mercedes touring car.

Note: army number plates on this car. and side screen.

Fig.72. Hitler in armoured 6-wheeled Mercedes
         touring car.

Note: army number plate.

Fig.73.   Hitler entering his car after inspecting
          guard of honour at Anhalter Bahnhof on his
          return from France, 1940.

SCHULZ aide-de-camp to Hitler, recently killed in Normandy and replaced as ADC by the

Fig. 74. Front view of Hitler's black Mercedes limousine.

Fig.75. Side of Hitler's black Mercedes limousine.

Hitler is seen leaving the British Embassy in Berlin after the conclusion of the talks with Mr. Eden and Sir John Simon in March 1935.

Fig.76. The Kolonne with Hitler in leading car alongside his driver KEMKA.

Fig.77.   The Kolonne with Hitler in back seat along-
          side HORTHY, the Regent of Hungary.

Fig.78.   The Kolonne with Hitler in leading car driving
          from the Anhalter Bahnhof to the Reichskanzlei
          on Hitler's return to Berlin from France July 1940.
Note: rosestrewn street.

<u>APPENDIX II - SCHLOSS KLESSHEIM.</u>

Schloss KLESSHEIM (Fig.79) is an 18th century mansion, built in the classical style and set in formal gardens; it is approached by a conspicuous double drive, entered through an elaborate brick wall gateway. To the south of the mansion, at a short distance, is a group of buildings which includes stables. To the north, between the house and the railway line lies a wood.

There are searchlight and light Flak positions in the immediate vicinity of the Schloss, 1000 yards north-east of which run railway sidings.

Schloss KLESSHEIM was first mentioned as Führerhauptquartier in January 1944. Whilst the Russian front held and Russia was the principal theatre of operations Führerhauptquartier (both at VINNITSA and ZHITOMIR) included the field headquarters of the Oberkommando der Wehrmacht. These headquarters were subsequently withdrawn with the advance of the Russian armies in Poland to RASTENBERG (East Prussia) - the former location of FHQ at the commencement of the Russian campaign. Although the furthest point to which the Russians have pressed the Germans back on the frontier of East Prussia is no more than 100 km. from RASTENBERG, this place is still apparently OKW for the Eastern front. OKW - Western front is probably located at MUNSINGEN near STUTTGART.

Fig.79.

The impossibility of accommodating the whole of FHQ, including the field headquarters of the OKW in this building is clearly indicated in the plan of Schloss Klessheim given in Fig.80. It is probable that, apart from its use for reception purposes it only accommodates that part of OKW which includes the WEHRMACHTFÜHRUNGSTAB (W.F.St.) or Armed Forces Operations Staff. At FHQ RASTENBERG W.E.St. totalled about 35 officers under JODL and WARLIMONT.

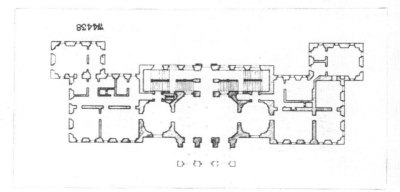

Fig.80.

It may also house that part of the Führerbegleitbataillon which is stationed at Schloss Klessheim (to protect this FHQ and the adjacent sidings, including the Führerzug).

The Führerbegleitbataillon consists of 4-6 companies. These include A.A. company, heavy company with armoured cars, and 2-4 motorised guard (Wach) companies. Its estimated strength is 1250. It is probable that the battalion has been split up and distributed among the various FHQs.

+ On such occasions as the Führer's birthday, e;g. 20th S April, 1944, when Hitler is reported to have received 200 generals at Schloss KLESSHEIM.

APPENDIX III - FOREIGN WORKERS IN SALZBURG AND DISTRICT.

The total number of foreign workers in the seven Austrian Gaue is estimated at 1,200,000 of whom probably about 100,000-150,000 are employed in and around Salzburg.

Whereas the more favoured foreign workers, e.g. French and Italians, were once frequently able to live in private lodgings, the influx into Salzburg and other Austrain towns of refugees from bombed German cities has caused this privilege to be withdrawn, and a decree of the local Gauleiter[+] of 18/1/1944 forbade hotel-keepers and other landlords to house male foreign workers or to renew the leases of rooms let to foreign tenants. Except in the case of domestic servants, workers in hotels, restaurants, and cafes, and labourers on isolated forms, it is likely that all foreign workers are now housed in communal camps (Gemeinschaftslager) in the Salzburg area.

Osterbeiter i.e. Russian and Ukrainian deportees and Ps/W constitute the great majority of foreign workers in Salzburg and district (HALLEIN for example). They include a large proportion of females, many of whom are employed as domestics in Salzburg itself. Others are employed on the railways as carriage cleaners, as at BERCHTESGADEN station for example. Like the Poles, they can be distinguished from other foreign workers by the badge they wear on the left breast of their overalls (Fig.81).

Fig.81.

Only second in number to the Ostarbeiter are the Poles, of whom about 15,000 are employed in Salzburg and its immediate vicinity (out of an estimated total of Poles in the whole of Austria of 200,000). Apart from agriculture and road con-struction, Poles in the Salzburg area are employed in textile mills, salt works, hydro-electric plants and on the railways, Polish workers being found at Salzburg station [x] as well as at BERCHTESGADEN station. Here Polish women are employed as carriage cleaners. Like the Ostarbeiter, the Poles are housed in camps where they are also fed separately from other inmates. Poles (and Ostarbeiter) may enter cafes but are not allowed to speak to Germans. They wear the badge shown in Fig.82 on the left breast of their overalls.

+ Dr. SCHEEL, Reichsstatthalter and Gauleiter, SALZBURG. Other
  notabilities at Salzburg: Gen. RINGEL, GOC Wehrkreis XVIII
                              SS Obersturmführer TRAUT i/c SD
                              Abschnitt, Salzburg.

x On night of 12/11/44 a French worker saw 3 Polish workers
  break off the seals of a Reichspostwagen. Clothes obtained
  in earlier thefts were found in their lodgings (Salzburger
  Zeitung 18/11/4).

Illustrations also shown in colour p. 166

Fig. 82.

The next most numerous nationality amongst foreign workers
is the <u>French</u>. These include deportees and Ps/W (prisonniers
de guerre transformes). They enjoy much better treatment than
Ostarbeiter or Poles and are allowed out at night until 10 or
11 o/c. In addition to the establishment of welfare offices
(Landesbauernschaft, Salzburg), the Nussdorferbar in the Franz-
Josef Strasse was recently turned over to the French as a
"foyer". Frenchmen (and women) are employed at Salzburg railway station, where the latter are entrusted with the washing
of the Party's special trains.

<u>Czech</u> foreign workers are also to be found in Salzburg
and district, a few being employed at Salzburg railway station.[+]
There are two Czech camps on the OBERSALZBERG, almost within
stone's throw of Hitler's residence.

Considerable numbers of <u>Italian</u> workers have been employed
at one time or another as railwaymen, waiters, and in factories,
etc. Like the French they receive favoured treatment.

Other nationalities found among the foreign worker
population include Croats, Serbs (at HALLEIN), Bulgarians,
Greeks, etc.

According to Russian sources, many foreign workers in
Austria have fled from their places of employment and formed
themselves into guerilla bands. Baldur v. SCHIRACH, the
Gauleiter for Austria, is reported to have issued orders in
July 1944 to every member of the Nazi Party "to hunt out the
thousands of foreign workers who have joined the guerillas".

[+] Three Czechs and a Croat employed as workers at Salzburg
railway station were sentenced to 2-4 years imprisonment
for theft (Salzburger Zeitung 13/2/44).

APPENDIX IV - ATTEMPT IN WEST PRUSSIA TO BLOW UP THE FÜHRERZUG.

The attempt was made in the autumn of 1941 on the railway between FREIDORF and SCHWARZWASSER by Polish saboteurs, whose orders, in point of fact, were to derail any fast train. It was therefore purely a matter of chance that the opportunity of destroying the Führer in his train presented itself. The detachment did, it is true, receive warning by radio from their HQ in West Prussia of the train's departure from KÖNIGS-BERG shortly after it had left. At that time Polish saboteurs were organised in detachments, every Kreis (district) having its detachment of 12 men, viz. wireless operator, six men for laying charges etc. and five men for local protection. Arms included machine pistols and revolvers. Communication was by short wave radio and each detachment had a set. This set was used not only for communicating with HQ and other detachments, but also for firing the charge. For some undisclosed reason the Führerzug stopped at a neighbouring station and another train was let through.

The several 1 kg. charges were laid some 20-30 mins. before the train was timed to pass, and were detonated by a current controlled by a receiving set which received the impress over the air from a short wave transmitter approximately 400 metres away from the line.

The resulting explosion is described as devasting, 430 Germans being killed and the line blocked for two days. The method of securing the charges to the rail and firing them is illustrated in Figs.83a,b and c below.

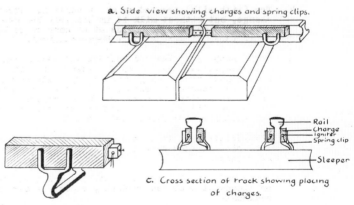

a. Side view showing charges and spring clips.

Rail
Charge
Igniter
Spring clip

Sleeper

b. Charge showing spring clip and igniter.

c. Cross section of track showing placing of charges.

Figs.83a,b and c.

APPENDIX V – "I" AS THE CLANDESTINE MEANS.

(see Part II - E).

"I" has been chosen as the most suitable medium, since its effect is not immediate like that of "R" or "F". In fact, taken in sufficiently small doses its symptons may not appear before 6 or 7 days. Under such circumstances there is no antidote.

Though a lethal dose (2 grams. in 2½ pints) taken at one and the same time might produce symptons (colic) the same day, the same quantity taken in cupfuls at a time in the morning, (Tea at breakfast) and the evening (coffee after dinner), would not occasion such symptons possibly for a day or two.

The delayed action of this medium is its chief advantage since it affords the best chance of the intended victim (Hitler) taking the necessary lethal quantity before suspicion has been aroused though any member of his entourage or of the train staff who has likewise taken beverages containing "I" may fall suddenly ill.

The characteristics of "I" are as follows:-

1. It is tasteless and odourless.

2. Neither hard nor soft water is visibly affected by the addition of one lethal dose (2 grams. to 2½ pints).

3. Black coffee treated with "I" in the same ratio indicates no perceptible change in appearance. Nor would the addition of milk make any immediate difference in the appearance of the beverage.

4. Tea (with milk) treated as above shows no detectable change, but without milk it immediately becomes opalescent and in the course of an hour or so becomes quite turbid and deposits a brown sediment.

5. Fruit such as apples and prunes, and vegetables (cabbage), stewed or boiled in water containing one lethal dose of "I" (2 grams.) to 2½ pints of water shows no abnormality campared with the same materials boiled in ordinary tap water. Though only insignif- icant quantities of "I" would be absorbed by the fruit or vegetable, the juice would be lethal.

6. The addition of "I" at the rate of one lethal dose to ½ pint of beer causes no alteration whatever in appearance.

7. Wines and spirits treated with "I" become turbid or cloudy at once and gradually deposit a dark brown sediment.

x x x x x x x x x x

Hitler, according to reliable information, is a tea addict. He always drinks it with milk. Since the milk is poured first into the cup, it is unlikely that the tea's opalescence (see 4. above) would be noticed as it came from the teapot.

Hitler is said to be extremely fond of apple juice.

The reports that he drinks enormous quantities of black coffee, which have appeared in the popular press from time to time, are denied by P/W who was body-servant to Hitler from 1936 to 1940, although a dining car attendant from von Ribbentrop's train declares this is not so and that he personally served the Führer with coffee (and milk) at the Berghof. Hitler may well have formed the habit in the course of the war.

Apart from such table waters as FACHINGER and APOLINARIS the only other beverage Hitler takes is his "near beer". This beer is said to be a special product of the HOLZKIRCHEN brewery, Munich, whose lorry makes a delivery once a month to the Berghof. (It is difficult to see how this beer could be treated outside the brewery, i.e. before bottling).

158

Colour Section

Topography of the Berchtesgaden area
Also shown in document sequence pp. 40–41

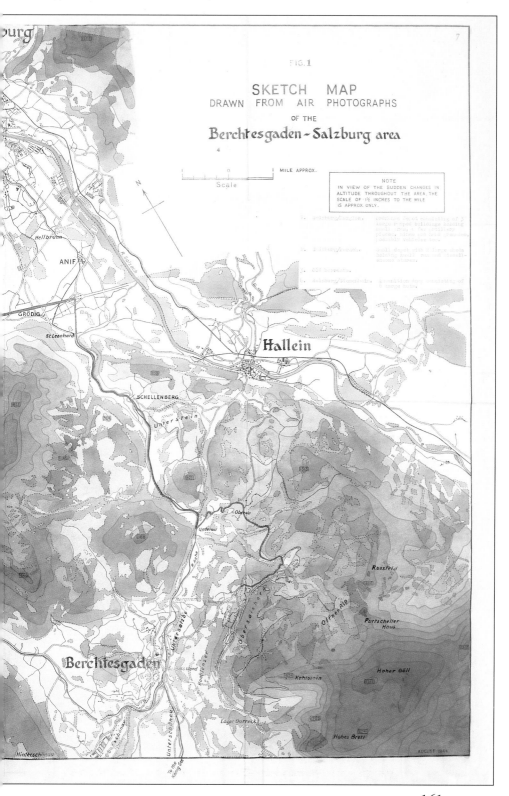

FIG. 1

SKETCH MAP
DRAWN FROM AIR PHOTOGRAPHS
OF THE
Berchtesgaden - Salzburg area

MILE APPROX.

Scale

NOTE
IN VIEW OF THE SUDDEN CHANGES IN
ALTITUDE THROUGHOUT THE AREA, THE
SCALE OF 1½ INCHES TO THE MILE
IS APPROX. ONLY.

AUGUST 1944

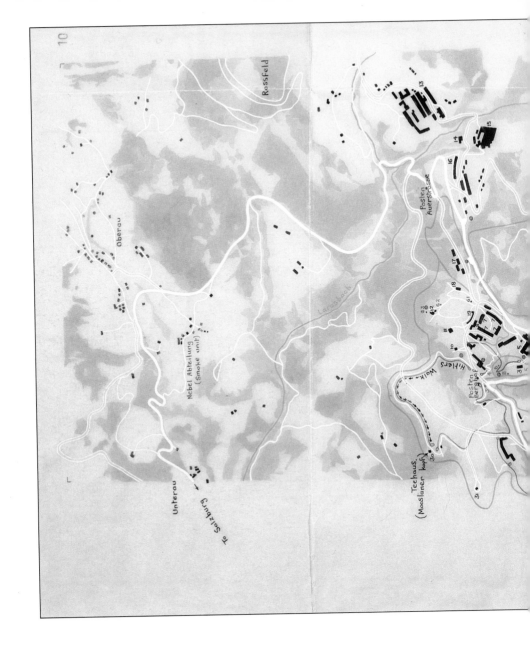

Topography of the Obersalzberg
Also shown in document sequence pp. 43–5

162

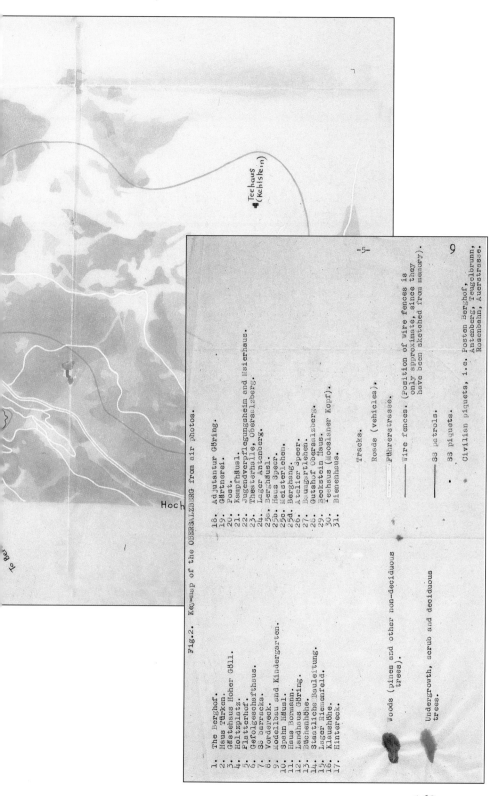

Fig.2. Key-map of the OBERSALZBERG from air photos.

1. The Berghof.
2. Haus Türken.
3. Gästehaus Hoher Göll.
4. Holzplatz.
5. Platterhof.
6. Gefolgschaftshaus.
7. SS barracks.
8. Vordereck.
9. Modellbau and Kindergarten.
10. Spahn Häusl.
11. Haus Bormann.
12. Landhaus Göring.
13. Bückenhöhe.
14. Staatliche Bauleitung.
15. Lager Riemenfeld.
16. Klaushöhe.
17. Hintereck.
18. Adjutantur Göring.
19. Gärtnerei.
20. Post.
21. Kampfhäusl.
22. Jugendverpflegungsheim and Maierhaus.
23. Theaterhalle, Obersalzberg.
24. Lager Antenberg.
25a. Berghäusl.
25b. Haus Speer.
25c. Meisterlehen.
25d. Berghang.
26. Atelier Speer.
27. Gutshof Obersalzberg.
28. Bauwärtlehen.
29. Beckstein Häus.
30. Teehaus (Mooslaner Kopf).
31. Bienenhaus.

Tracks.

Roads (vehicles).

Führerstrasse.

Wire fences. (Position of wire fences is only approximate, since they have been sketched from memory).

SS patrols.

SS piquets.

Civilian piquets, i.e. Posten Berghof, Antenberg, Teugelbrunn, Rosenbahn, Auerstrasse.

Woods (pines and other non-deciduous trees).

Undergrowth, scrub and deciduous trees.

Teehaus (Kehlstein)

Hoch

-5-

9

*Uniforms worn by security personnel
at the Obersalzberg*
Also shown in document sequence
pp. 89, 91

165

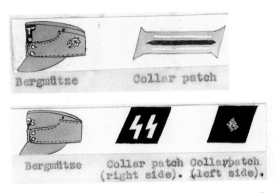

Disguise: converting Gebirgsjäger (top) to SS (bottom) uniforms
Also shown in document sequence p. 110

Badges worn by foreign workers in the Salzburg area
Also shown in document sequence pp. 154, 155